'How wonderful – finally a passionate and scholarly yet practical book focusing solely on the pivotal importance of adults understanding and developing empathy in very young children. Helen Garnett has contributed an exciting seminal book which deserves very serious attention from the world of early years practitioners and parents. It is a rare creature – a book that balances excellent research into empathy with excellent practical ways of putting all the ideas into practice. It is a "must-have" for all people wanting the best future for children.'

– Jenny Mosley, author, Early Years Consultant and
former Lecturer in Education

'This is the perfect book for early years practitioners who want to better understand the importance of empathy.'

– Dr Suzanne Zeedyk, Development Psychologist,
Research Scientist and Founder of connected baby

'People have mixed feelings about empathy. That's just one of the unsettling arguments in this important and timely book from Helen Garnett. Evidently, there's more interest in empathy than ever before but too little of it around. Empathy is the capacity to understand and respond to the feelings of others. Like all human capacities, empathy is not evenly distributed and it needs to be cultivated. This is one of the vital roles of parenting and of education. Too often empathy is in the sidelines in education: one of a mixed bag of so-called "soft-skills" – worthy in themselves, no doubt, but low priority compared to the relentless pursuit of academic success. Helen Garnett sets out in plain language why these priorities are wrong. She and her co-contributors explain concisely the different forms of empathy and why they should be at the heart of education from the earliest years. And they offer practical guidelines for how to do that. Academic work is often associated with 'higher order' thinking skills and it's commonly thought that these are what make us distinctively human. Helen Garnett's compelling account of empathy and compassion makes it clear that the higher order capacities of feeling could hardly be more important in holding together our relationships, our communities and in an essential sense, our shared humanity. This is a powerful, passionate and practical appeal to humanize education for the sake of all of our children.'

– *Sir Ken Robinson, Educator and*
New York Times *best-selling author*

DEVELOPING EMPATHY IN THE EARLY YEARS

of related interest

Inclusion, Play and Empathy
Neuroaffective Development in Children's Groups
Edited by Susan Hart
Foreword by Phyllis Booth
ISBN 978 1 78592 006 6
eISBN 978 1 78450 243 0

Nurturing Personal, Social and Emotional
Development in Early Childhood
A Practical Guide to Understanding Brain Development
and Young Children's Behaviour
Debbie Garvey
Foreword by Dr Suzanne Zeedyk
ISBN 978 1 78592 223 7
eISBN 978 1 78450 500 4

Listening to Young Children, Expanded Third Edition
A Guide to Understanding and Using the Mosaic Approach
Alison Clark
Foreword by Peter Moss
ISBN 978 1 90939 122 2
eISBN 978 1 90939 126 0

Promoting Young Children's Emotional Health and Wellbeing
A Practical Guide for Professionals and Parents
Sonia Mainstone-Cotton
ISBN 978 1 78592 054 7
eISBN 978 1 78450 311 6

Cyril Squirrel Finds Out About Love
Jane Evans
Illustrated by Izzy Bean
ISBN 978 1 78592 080 6
eISBN 978 1 78450 341 3

DEVELOPING EMPATHY IN THE EARLY YEARS

A Guide for Practitioners

HELEN GARNETT

With additional material by JACKIE HARLAND,
HELEN LUMGAIR and VALERIE LOVEGREEN

Jessica Kingsley *Publishers*
London and Philadelphia

First published in 2018
by Jessica Kingsley Publishers
73 Collier Street
London N1 9BE, UK
and
400 Market Street, Suite 400
Philadelphia, PA 19106, USA

www.jkp.com

Library of Congress Cataloging in Publication Data
A CIP catalog record for this book is available from the Library of Congress

British Library Cataloguing in Publication Data
A CIP catalogue record for this book is available from the British Library

ISBN 978 1 78592 143 8
eISBN 978 1 78450 418 2

Printed and bound in Great Britain

Contents

Introduction

Our preschools are full of tomorrow's people. They are the parents and teachers, workers and leaders of our future world. Difficult decisions and tough challenges will face them. Effective parenting and leadership will require personal resilience, openness to change and a fundamental understanding of the human experience.

If our children are to flourish in tomorrow's world, they will need complete emotional and empathetic 'tool kits'. Not only do we need to empower them by teaching them about identifying, legitimising and processing feelings, we also need to establish and model healthy relationships, demonstrating empathy and responsiveness to each other.

Empathy, quite simply, doesn't grow on trees. It grows organically, incrementally. It is caught, not taught. We are not able to pass it on if we have not first received it. Empathy takes root when people stop to consider, reflect on and understand other people's feelings and behaviours. It flourishes when we learn to understand and appreciate their perspectives. Empathy becomes established when individuals take the trouble to work each other out.

Empathy is in decline. We are in the midst of an 'empathy deficit.' Around-the-clock convenience is currently in vogue and we are at risk of becoming increasingly resistant to any further disruption of our comfortable lives. We are responding less to the suffering of others and more to our own needs.

We simply aren't making the same sort of effort as we used to. We don't need to go to the bank; we can send a payment online. We don't need to visit our relatives in person, we can Skype them. We don't need to ring our friends; we can simply 'message' them.

Empathy is effortful. It requires us to stop and think. It demands space and time. Our world has countless numbers of people who are governed by unregulated feelings and bound by their unawareness of other people's perspectives and behaviours. In return, they are misjudged and misunderstood, largely due to a lack of empathy. Day by day we try to patch up these broken individuals – in our education system, in psychiatric care and in our prisons – but it is often far too late.

There are no bad kids, just impressionable, conflicted young people wrestling with emotions and impulses, trying to communicate their feelings and needs the only way they know how.[1]

Early years education is the period of time when emotional intelligence and empathy are either planted and tended to, or neglected and untended, even uprooted.

When a whole school approach is empathetic, there is a very real chance for meaningful and lifelong empathy to develop. This book explores the power of planting empathy in our early years teaching and classrooms.

Chapter 1 explores the historical background of both individual and global empathy, and the essential role that a whole school empathetic approach can play in the early years classroom.

Chapter 2 explains affective and cognitive empathy in detail, along with the effects of emotional contagion. It provides helpful strategies for creating a culture of cognitive empathy, underpinned by recent research on the skills that precede empathy.

In Chapter 3, Jackie Harland explores the development of theory of mind, and how to test the children for it in your setting. This is one of the most important areas of development in a child's life and is a topic noticeably neglected in early years training to date.

Chapter 4 looks at pedagogy, demonstrating how it is that early years practitioners, in developing their own philosophy of teaching, are instrumental in building powerful empathetic practices from the ground up.

Chapter 5 unearths the vital components of an emotionally healthy classroom. Early years practitioners are given relevant and helpful strategies to support young children in recognising, processing and regulating the myriad of feelings, impulses and behaviours they experience.

Chapter 6 is an innovative look at conflict and how essential it is for a child to experience it, and then to learn how to resolve it. The chapter reveals how healthy conflict essentially increases our emotional health and empathy levels.

Chapter 7 examines the central role of positive language in the joint development of our emotional and cognitive abilities and empathy skills. Without the presence of positive language, the brain lacks vital 'wiring', and children will suffer as a result, both emotionally and academically.

Chapter 8 reveals how pretend play is central to the nurturing of empathy, through turn-taking, sharing and problem-solving skills, and how it builds vital understanding of the different perspectives and attitudes of others.

In Chapter 9, Helen Lumgair throws a spotlight on how stories facilitate the developing skills of perspective taking and critical thinking, alongside empathetic actions. She explores narrative and demonstrates what a powerful vehicle it is in the growth of empathy and responsiveness.

In Chapter 10, Valerie Lovegreen takes a look at social cognition, an essential tool in early learning and thinking. She describes how children can learn to think as individuals and as a community through forming a community of inquiry. Such shared thinking leads to empathy in action.

Finally, Chapter 11 uncovers the mystery of autism, explaining it in such a way that practitioners can embrace working with children with autism with increased understanding and empathy.

If we always do what we always did, we will always get what we always got.[2]

It's time to do it differently. Pick up the empathy baton and run the empathy race. Kind and considerate children are developed where kindness and consideration are practised. Tolerant and cooperative children thrive in an environment where tolerance and cooperation are evident. Future parents and leaders are built where shared thinking and collaborative learning are valued.

Plant empathy! Sow it deep into the ground, the pedagogy of your preschool.

Plant it in the way you set out the physical environment. Plant it in the daily schedule, giving children time to plan and play. Plant it in your story times and in your role-play areas. Plant it in your shared thinking and scaffolding. Plant it in your body language and in the words you speak. Plant it in your observations and assessments. Above all, plant it in the day-to-day, habitual routines of the setting.

It is only when we make the crucial decision to place empathy at the centre of our practice that we will begin to witness a shift in its decline. When empathy is tangible and visible, and when we openly and lovingly deliver an education of the heart as well as of the mind, we grow empathetic children and a hopeful future.

It really is that simple.

Notes

1. Lansbury, J. (2014) *No Bad Kids: Toddler Discipline Without Shame.* CreateSpace Independent Publishing Platform, p.6.
2. Adapted from Albert Einstein, 1879–1955, German physicist.

CHAPTER ONE

Empathy in the 21st Century

The challenge of understanding another person and what it takes to truly feel understood by another is at the hub of human social existence.[1]

Personal empathy

Empathy is the imaginative act of stepping into the shoes of another person and understanding their feelings and perspectives. That makes it very different from sympathy, which is an emotional response, such as pity or feeling sorry for someone, that does not involve trying to grasp their view point or experiences.[2]

To put it simply, empathy is stepping inside another person, living in their world, looking through their eyes and understanding their history. It requires us to make an effort.

Richard Gere, actor, said this after he went undercover as a homeless man in New York City:

No one noticed me. I felt what it was like to be a homeless man. People would just pass by me and look at me in disgrace. Only one lady was kind enough to give me some food. It was an experience I'll never forget. So many times we forget how blessed we are. We should not take that for granted. And if we can help someone in need, we should.

Patricia Moore, an industrial designer, was horrified by the attitude of her colleagues towards people with arthritis. 'We don't design for those people,' she heard them say. And so, in the mid-1970s, Patricia dressed up as an 85-year-old woman to see what it was like to be old. She wore fogged up glasses, simulated arthritis by binding up her hands and feet, and wore shoes that were uneven. Based on her experiences, she has become a campaigner for senior citizens. In addition, she has also created some products designed especially for people who have arthritis, such as rubber-handled potato peelers that are now to be found in most kitchens. You probably have one!

George Orwell, author, dressed up as a tramp in the late 1920s and early 1930s and wandered around London, meeting up with beggars and tramps. Here was a man who had been to Eton, who had served as an officer out in India, wanting to 'taste' other people's lives. After his experience he said that he would 'never again think that all tramps are drunken scoundrels, nor expect a beggar to be grateful when I give him a penny'.[3]

With each of these examples, there was a full immersion into the life of another. These people were willing to experience a different perspective and gain new insights. Consequently, their preconceptions were challenged. Their viewpoints changed. No longer did they feel judgemental. They understood.

This is the essence of empathy: to truly understand another's viewpoint simply because you made the effort to understand who he is.

Global empathy

In 1206, Giovanni Bernadone, the son of a wealthy cloth merchant, went on a pilgrimage to Rome, and was so moved by the plight of a beggar outside St Peter's Basilica that he swapped places with the tramp and spent the day begging for alms. This appeared to be a turning point for him. Following on from this he founded a religious order, giving to the poor and lepers. He went on to become Saint Francis of Assisi. He once said, 'Where there is charity and wisdom, there is neither fear nor ignorance.' It is the combined effect of 'charity and wisdom' that is empathy in action.

To understand empathy, we need to use our imagination, to adopt other people's agonies, and to make them our own. One of the most important examples of this involved the Quakers, a religious movement based in Pennsylvania, America. The Quakers were keen to switch on people's affective empathy (not that it had such a title at the time) towards the appalling treatment of slaves. They used shocking posters of a slave ship, overcrowded, dark and hideously cramped. People were horrified. The visual brutality stirred them. The Quakers took former slaves around the country, and these slaves talked about the treatment they'd experienced; about being whipped, or being hooked onto cranes with heavy weights hanging from their feet. Together, they showed the public the instruments of torture, the iron collars and the force-feeding instruments used to prevent slaves from their pitiful attempts at dying of undernourishment, a death preferable to the appalling existence they suffered. Tens of thousands of people were shocked to the core, protesting at the appalling treatment of slaves.

This triggered petitions and boycotts. One woman even visited around 3000 households, asking them not to eat slave-grown sugar. William Wilberforce, over half a century later, said this in his Abolition Speech of 1789:

> I verily believe therefore, if the wretchedness of any one of the many hundred Negroes stowed in each ship could be brought before their [the Liverpool merchants'] view, and remain within the sight of the African Merchant, that there is no one among them whose heart would bear it.

Only when people see themselves in the same 'shackles and chains' can there follow a profound change in thinking. We have to recognise the pain, and understand it, in order to empathise fully with another's plight.

Another group famous for their empathy was the Victorians. This was clearly demonstrated by the various Factory Acts and the Chimney Sweeps Act, all of which reduced or abolished certain cruel or harsh activities, and of course culminated in the Abolition of Slavery Act in 1833.

The first half of the 20th century saw a continued rise in empathy. Two World Wars and the development of mass media made us painfully aware of the atrocities and suffering that accompany war and conflict. Genocides, revolutions and a callous disregard for human rights have filled our newspapers and television screens for decades.

These days we see people walking miles in the middle of the night to raise money for cancer research, or sleeping rough in aid of the homeless. Others swim the channel, alone or in human shoals. Some climb mountains or walk to the North Pole in aid of charity. People search high and low for answers to world poverty or cruelty, often on the front line of whatever it is that appals and moves them. They have seen the atrocities, the pain, the desperation of another person, and they want to take action. This type of collaborative empathy has huge implications and impact on both political and social change. It births transformation, and even revolution.

And yet there is a general lack of compassion here in the West. As refugees pour into Europe, desperate to escape from a terrorist regime, as floods wipe away entire neighbourhoods, the West watches briefly, sends a text to donate some money, before settling back to enjoy a football match or an evening with friends.

A recent report backed by organisations including Oxfam and Friends of the Earth says this:

> The values that must be strengthened – values that are commonly held and which can be brought to the fore – include: empathy towards those who are facing the effects of humanitarian and environmental crises, concern for future generations, and recognition that human prosperity resides in

relationships – both with one another and with the natural world.[4]

Global empathy, our compassion for people all over this world, is as important as our compassion for the people around us. Empathy, it seems, is one of the most effective tools of history; it is the foundation of all of our shared values. Its impact is huge, and its legacy is priceless.

In short, we can't live without it.

The trouble is, we think that we can.

The scientific foundations of empathy

The word 'empathy' was coined in 1909 from the German word 'einfühlung' meaning 'feeling into'. Prior to this, the closest word to empathy was 'sympathy', which is loosely described as feeling sorrow for other people's troubles and adversities.

Empathy can be neatly divided into three categories, all essentially interlinked:

- **Affective empathy**: this refers to the different feelings we get when we respond to other people and their emotions. We may either mirror or share in other people's feelings.

- **Cognitive empathy**: this is when we see the other person's perspective. We are able to put ourselves in the shoes of another person by identifying and understanding those emotions.

- **Empathic concern**: this is when we recognise and are in tune with someone else's emotional state, and can feel and show concern. This is when we take action.

Empathy is an innate trait. One hundred per cent of us possess it. Ninety-eight per cent of us use it but only a small percentage of us reach our full empathetic potential. Roughly 2 per cent of the population have empathy but not all of its parts and as a result, their empathy is restricted or non-existent. Human beings have always had this trait. It is a basic characteristic of the human species, with many physiological reactions and processes that accompany it. Recent research suggests that there is even a 'fundamental baseline' of empathy among mammals. Rats get distressed when they see another rat in pain.[5] Rhesus monkeys will stop operating a device for getting food if this caused another monkey to get an electric shock.[6] Our survival depends upon it. If we constantly seek self-interest over empathy, our survival as a species will be threatened. We need to be sensitive to our offspring and our 'group'.

Recent research into the science of empathy is flagging up new and exciting findings, the sort of findings that are currently having, and will continue to have, a huge impact on our teaching of empathy.

First, in the early 1990s, was the significant discovery of mirror neurons.[7] These are a type of brain cell that 'fire' or respond equally when we perform an action, or when we see someone else performing that same action. The implications of this simple concept are mind blowing. Up till this point, scientists believed that we used thinking processes to interpret or predict other people's behaviour or actions. This is not the case. Our mirror neurons fire up when we see other people's actions and facial expressions, and we immediately experience the feeling associated with that action. There is no thought process involved.

The mirror neuron system influences our ability to empathise by adopting the other person's point of view. For example, the mirror neurons fire up when we see another person smiling and we 'feel' their smile. Through the mirror neurons we start to understand the mental state of another person, a crucial element of empathy. This was a game changer in neuroscience, and in the understanding of empathy. A leading professor of psychology and neuroscience said this about the discovery:

The discovery of mirror neurons in the frontal lobes of monkeys, and their potential relevance to human brain evolution is the single most important 'unreported' (or at least, unpublicised) story of the decade. I predict that mirror neurons will do for psychology what DNA did for biology: they will provide a unifying framework and help explain a host of mental abilities that have hitherto remained mysterious and inaccessible to experiments.[8]

Next was the discovery of certain brains cells called spindle cells. They were discovered a hundred years or so ago, and no one paid much attention to them. But then, in the 1990s, a graduate student working with Patrick Hof, a professor of neuroscience, spotted some brain cells that were rather large, and had long spindle-shaped bodies, looking rather like tall, thin, purple bananas! There didn't seem to be very many of them, but because they were so unusually big it seemed that they might be doing something rather important. They were! Patrick Hof discovered that these cells were vital in the processing of emotions and therefore played an important role in empathy. The spindle cells seem to send signals simultaneously to both the emotional and thinking part of the brain. Empathy, it seems, begins with a thought, and connects with a feeling of sadness, happiness, and so on. Spindle cells effectively broadcast this content to the rest of the brain, allowing us to connect emotionally with each other.

What is more, it has been discovered that these spindle cells have some 'degeneration' in people with alexithymia, the term used to describe nearly 10 per cent of the population who have a deficit in their emotional awareness. People with dementia and autism are part of this group.

Up next was a study in 2009,[9] where 200 people took tests that effectively measured how good they were at identifying and feeling other people's emotions. These people were also asked to give samples of their DNA. The DNA was required in order to measure the difference in the three types of gene that is the receptor of oxytocin, fondly known as the 'love hormone'. (People have one of three variations of this gene.) What the researchers found was that those people with one particular type of gene scored higher on the tests of empathy than the other two gene types.

In other words, some people are going to find it easier to understand other people because of their genes. This could be bad news for those people who have the genes with less empathy potential but Sarina Rodrigues, who carried out the research, had this to say on the subject:

> Our genes give us a natural predisposition to the way we might want to socially connect with people or handle stress but through nurturing and social connectivity and understanding, people can overcome these obstacles.[10]

In 2013[11] there was another breakthrough. It was discovered that there is a part of the brain that recognises a lack of empathy, and then corrects it. This part of the brain is called the right supramarginal gyrus. It is the same part that helps us work out our own emotional state and how it differs from the state of people around us. What the researchers also discovered was that when this part of the brain doesn't work properly, or when we have to make a very quick decision, our ability for empathy is dramatically reduced. Empathy, it seems, needs time and effort to reach its potential.

What emerges from all of these studies is an understanding that our empathy levels are highly dependent on our brain chemistry, and brain chemistry depends on our nurturing environment. Children who receive little or no nurturing or empathy will be unable to 'read' other people. This is not just a massive disadvantage for them. It is a tragedy.

Empathy's decline

Empathy is getting more public attention now than at any other time in our history. Over the last ten years the frequency of Internet searches for empathy has literally doubled. There is a deep interest in what it is, why we need it and how to 'learn' it. We are at the heights of an empathy uprising. There appears to be a growing, global recognition that empathy holds the building blocks to world peace.

There is an extraordinary paradox here. While empathy is becoming increasingly popular to study and examine, at the same time its presence in the lives of young adults, adolescents and children appears to be on the wane, causing what is now known as an 'empathy deficit'.

Roman Krznaric, writer and cultural thinker, believes that there is a growing empathy deficit across the Western world, with the steepest fall taking place over the last ten years. Barack Obama, in a speech made in 2006, talked about the 'empathy deficit' in the USA as being more significant than the federal deficit. Empathy, it seems, is being closely examined through a global microscope and has been found fundamentally lacking.

What is the proof of this? How do we know?

A 2010 study[12] has shown that college students in the USA are not as empathetic as college students in the 1980s and 90s. This study began in 1979, when a survey was carried out involving nearly 14,000 college students. Seventy-one identical surveys have followed over the following thirty years. Initially there were no significant contrasts to report. And then suddenly, around 2004, there was a sudden and sharp drop in empathy. At the same time, there was a noticeable rise in narcissism.

The area of empathy that showed a marked decline was cognitive empathy: the ability we have to understand how someone else is feeling. But more worrying than that, there was also a marked drop in emotional (affective) empathy, which is the actual response to someone else's pain or distress. Between 1979 and 2009, such empathetic concern had dropped by 48 per cent.

The results have given rise to much speculation. Is it the endless exposure to the horrors of war, famine and natural disasters on the television or in the newspapers? Is it an increase in social isolation? Is it the influence of social media? Is it the high level of violence shown in movies or in video games? Is it the increasingly convenient world we live in? Is it our consumer society, where everything is expendable? Or is it because we live in a culture that positively discourages empathy, 'a culture that too often tells us our principal goal in life is to be rich, thin, young, famous, safe, and entertained'?[13]

Whatever the speculations, one thing is clear. At the beginning of the 21st century, when new millennium students took part in the same survey, it was evident that something critical had happened in order to alter the empathy levels of an entire generation of students.

The speculations go on and on, but one thing is clear: empathy is on the wane. We are responding less to other people's suffering. In addition, our ability to acknowledge different perspectives has significantly altered. While we may understand other viewpoints, we are not acting in the best interests of them. We are becoming less empathetic and more indifferent.

So, what can we do about it?

Empathy in the 21st-century classroom

Human beings have many needs and Maslow's hierarchy of needs puts it simply (see Figure 1.1). We start with basic needs such as air, water and food. Then we have our needs for safety, which include protection from the elements, security, law and order. Next we have our social needs such as love, friendship and intimacy. Following that, we need esteem: achievement, self-respect and respect from others. And finally, right at the top, we have our personal growth, the realisation of our potential and our self-fulfilment. Hidden among all these needs is empathy, packed tightly among safety, love, self-respect and intimacy.

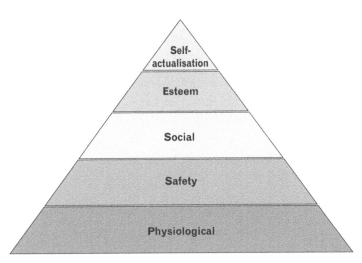

Figure 1.1 Maslow's hierarchy of needs

Despite being referred to as a 'soft skill', empathy is crucial for our mental health. Empathy:

> allows us to create bonds of trust, it gives us insights into what others may be feeling or thinking; it helps us understand how or why others are reacting to situations, it sharpens our 'people acumen' and it informs our decisions.[14]

In short, empathy creates connections between people and brings them together. It is at the core of pro-social behaviour.

Schools must put relationships at the heart of their education programme. Our feelings give us valuable information about our needs. If we don't give names to these feelings, then we can't assign meaning to them. If we can't assign meaning to them, then how can we use these feelings as the essential guides for the relationships in our lives?

Sir Ken Robinson, international advisor on education, says that when discussing schools we must:

> connect with each other through the power of empathy, through the power of intuition and mutuality and that all

of those things get lost in an industrialised, homogenised, atomised system of education, and the price couldn't be higher, and we're paying for it every day in disaffection, disengagement, and emotional turmoil.[15]

He believes that our education system has not evolved from a model that is now out of date. Our schools are organised along factory lines with our children educated in 'batches', with standardised testing. Empathy has little or no place in these buildings or systems.

Rabbi Michael Lerner, political activist, also has a clear vision of empathy in schools. One of his ideas is that schools must stop spinning out children and their qualifications as if they were one and the same thing, and start producing schools that nurture empathy. This nurturing must not be seen as an added 'extra', but should be the very foundation of learning, the bottom line of education. He has seen first-hand that schools that allow children to mentor (show empathy) and tutor the younger children have a significant effect.

A school in NYC had adopted this technique and the results were phenomenal. The older children felt responsible for the younger ones and were there to help them with their homework and school-related projects. The cooperation and camaraderie between them encouraged a friendlier and more harmonious school environment. It helped build the character traits that bring about empathy.[16]

This may seem obvious. And surely our schools are doing this already? In most cases, they are but more often than not as a 'soft skill' as opposed to the 'bottom line' philosophy. Our schools are seemingly keen for change, for reform, for raising standards. There is a gradual realisation that empathy needs to take more of a centre stage in children's learning journeys. Social and emotional education is now being threaded into national curriculums, and awareness is rising all the time.

But empathy still isn't at the heart of learning. This 'heart' has to consist of the formation of strong and lasting friendships between practitioners, children and families where practitioners themselves are models of empathy. Martin Hoffman, a professor of psychology at New York University, has these punchy words to say on the subject: 'You can enhance empathy by the way you treat children, or you can kill it by providing a harsh punitive environment.'[17]

The decline in empathy can cause us to feel pessimistic. However, if empathy levels can go down, they can also go up. There is no doubt about it; a revolution is happening, an empathy revolution. Thanks to a tsunami of research into the science of empathy, new and exciting insights on the topic are being uncovered year on year. Books are being written, and recent research continues to unravel this fascinating human trait. We know that we can 'grow' empathy in our children and in ourselves. Furthermore, it makes sound economic, social and emotional sense to start fostering empathy at the earliest stages of education. It will, quite literally, save us a fortune.

Children's social problems in the UK currently cost us £17 billion a year[18] including £5 billion spent on children in care, £4 billion spent on benefits for 18–24-year-olds, and another £900 million spent on mental health issues or alcohol or drug problems. This is utter madness. Early intervention works. Late intervention 'rarely turns lives round'.[19]

The Good Childhood Report of 2016 found worrying age and gender differences in well-being among children. Girls were increasingly unhappy with their appearance and with life in general. 'England ranked last out of fifteen countries for happiness with appearance and also had the most pronounced gender differences of all participating countries.'[20]

The Dalai Lama says, 'Only the development of compassion and understanding for others can bring the tranquillity and happiness we all seek.'

Is this idealistic and unworkable?

Seemingly not! Research shows that empathy reduces prejudice and racism, fights inequality and creates peace.[21] Research also demonstrates how empathy deepens intimacy, boosts relationships,[22] reduces bullying,[23] promotes heroic acts[24] and even succeeds where brutality fails.[25]

Empathy calms, soothes and placates. While it may not be the panacea to cure everything – it may be the best possible place to start.

The words of Pope Francis sum it up beautifully:

'This capacity for empathy leads to a genuine encounter – we have to progress toward this culture of encounter – in which heart speaks to heart. We are enriched by the wisdom of the other and become open to travelling together the path to greater understanding, friendship and solidarity.'

Travelling this path together entails listening to the wisdom of the children and creating a respectful friendship. It means extending this friendship to colleagues and parents. Children who learn to forge good relationships in preschools tend to thrive at school and beyond. Classrooms that practise empathy create a safe space, where vulnerability is acknowledged as a learning asset.[26] Empathetic classrooms encourage children to express themselves emotionally, so that they become emotionally 'competent'. Empathetic classrooms lead by example. Empathy is not a trait that can be learned in isolation, or developed in a vacuum. It is observed, copied, observed again and practised.

One of the crucial factors in creating an empathetic environment is the elimination of stress. There is a strong correlation between an awareness of our own minds and our ability to empathise. In order for this awareness to flourish, the environment needs to be peaceful, allowing children the time and space for healthy action and reflection. 'Creaticide' is a new word describing the 'national design to kill literary, scientific and mathematical creativity' in schools and underlines the current pressure in delivering 'successful' testing to children of all ages. Testing becomes the product, rather than the process of learning. Opportunities for creativity are stripped away, not because there is no time, but because teachers are more worried about the testing results. This puts the young child under considerable pressure to pay attention, rather than following their interests. As J.P. Guilford put it back in 1950, 'The child is under pressure to conform for the sake of economy and for the sake of satisfying prescribed standards.'

Environments that implement social and emotional learning and mindfulness foster personal, social and academic success. Recent studies support these findings; social and emotional learning (SEL) programmes increased academic performance (by an 11-percentile-point gain in achievement), along with positive attitudes and behaviours, and reduced aggression and emotional distress.[27]

Despite this host of evidence, many schools continue to embrace increased academisation at an increasingly younger age. This does not allow for the process of reflection and the development of personal awareness.

Such pressure causes stress for both child and teacher, and is the underlying cause for anxiety in classrooms all around the world. Unwanted behaviour in the classroom builds. A huge surge in attention deficit hyperactivity disorder (ADHD) over the last twenty years potentially owes much of its growth to such academic emphasis. No wonder there are unwanted behaviours in classrooms. Undesirable conduct is almost always due to unmet needs and a lack of understanding.

Let's start to unravel these needs by practising empathy. Let's save our nations a fortune and create a culture of understanding. Let's grow emotional health in our young children. Let's dedicate ourselves to developing empathy and, in doing so, buy us hope for future generations.

Too often we underestimate the power of a touch, a smile, a kind word, a listening ear, an honest compliment, or the smallest act of caring, all of which have the potential to turn a life around.[28]

And that is our mission of empathy. To turn lives around.

Notes

1. Yaniv, D. (2012) 'Dynamics of creativity and empathy in role reversal: Contributions from neuroscience.' *Review of General Psychology 16*, 1, 70–77, p.70. Used by kind permission of Dani Yaniv.
2. Krznaric, R. (2014) 'My children became my greatest teachers.' *The Guardian*, 25 January. Courtesy of Guardian News and Media.
3. Orwell, G. (1933) *Down and Out in Paris and London*. London: Victor Gollancz.
4. Crompton, T. (2010) *Common Cause: The Case for Working with our Cultural Values*. WWF-UK. Accessed on 26/06/2017 at http://assets.wwf.org.uk/downloads/common_cause_report.pdf.
5. Church, R.M. (1959) 'Emotional reactions of rats to the pain of others.' *Journal of Comparative and Physiological Psychology 52*, 132–134.
6. Masserman, J.H., Wechkin, S. and Terris, W. (1964) 'Altruistic behaviour in rhesus monkeys.' *The American Journal of Psychiatry 121*, 584–585.
7. Rizzolatti, G., Fadiga, L., Gallese, V. and Fogassi, L. (1996) 'Premotor cortex and the recognition of motor actions.' *Brain 119*, 593–609.
8. Ramachandran, V.S. (2000) 'Mirror neurons and imitation learning as the driving force behind the great leap forward in human evolution.' Accessed on 26/06/2017 at www.edge.org/conversation/mirror-neurons-and-imitation-learning-as-the-driving-force-behind-the-great-leap-forward-in-human-evolution.
9. Rodrigues, S.M., Saslow, L.R., Garcia, N., John, O.P. and Keltner, D. (2009) 'Oxytocin receptor genetic variation related to empathy and stress reactivity in humans.' *Proceedings of the National Academy of Science of the United States of America 106*, 21437–21441.
10. Marsh, J. (2009) 'The unselfish gene?' *Greater Good Magazine*, March 2009. Berkeley, CA: The Greater Good Science Center at UC Berkeley. Accessed on 27/07/2017 at https://greatergood.berkeley.edu/article/item/the_unselfish_gene.
11. Silani, G., Lamm, C., Ruff, C.C. and Singer, T. (2013) 'Right supermarginal gyrus is crucial to overcome emotional egocentricity bias in social judgements.' *Journal of Neuroscience 33*, 39, 15466–15476.
12. Konrath, S.H., O'Brien, E.H. and Hsing, C. (2010) 'Changes in dispositional empathy in American college students over time: a meta-analysis.' *Personality and Social Psychology Review 15*, 2, 180–198.
13. Barack Obama to Northwestern University graduates at 2006 Commencement.
14. Martinuzzi, B. (2009) 'The leader as a mensch: Become the kind of person others want to follow.' Six Seconds Emotional Intelligence Press, p.20.
15. Robinson, K. (2011) Educating the Heart and Mind. Dalai Lama Center Speakers Series.
16. Kuehnert, J.S. (2014) 'Empathy: Is it teachable?' Academic Exchange: A blog by Academic Credentials Evaluation Institute, Inc. (ACEI), 10 July 2014. Accessed on 27/07/2017 at https://acei-global.blog/2014/07/10/empathy-is-it-teachable.

17. Szalavitz, M. (2010) 'How not to raise a bully: The early roots of empathy.' *Time Magazine*, 17 April. Accessed at http://content.time.com/time/health/article/0,8599,1982190,00.html, on 27 July 2017. Used by kind permission of Martin Hoffmann.

18. Chowdray, H. and Oppenheim, C. (2015) *Spending on Late Intervention: How We Can Do Better for Less*. London: Early Intervention Foundation. Accessed on 27/07/2017 at www.eif.org.uk/wp-content/uploads/2015/02/SPENDING-ON-LATE-INTERVENTION.pdf.

19. Chowdray and Oppenhiem (2015).

20. The Children's Society (2016) *The Good Childhood Report 2016: Summary*. The Children's Society. Accessed on 26/06/2017 at www.childrenssociety.org.uk/sites/default/files/pcr090_summary_web.pdf.

21. Todd, A.R., Bodenhausen, G.V., Richeson, J.A. and Galinsky, A.D. (2011) 'Perspective taking combats automatic expressions of racial bias.' *Journal of Personality and Social Psychology 100*, 6, 1027–1042.

22. Block-Lerner, J., Adair, C., Plumb, J.C., Rhatigan, D.L. and Orsillo, S.M. (2007) 'The case for mindfulness-based approaches in the cultivation of empathy: Does nonjudgmental, present-moment awareness increase capacity for perspective-taking and empathic concern?' *Journal of Marital and Family Therapy 33*, 501–516.

23. Smith, M.L., Alleva, R. and Linehan, T. (2012) The Courage to Care Program. Accessed on 11/08/2017 at www.courage2care.net.

24. Oliner, S.P. and Oliner, P. (1992) *Altruistic Personality: Rescuers of Jews In Nazi Europe*. New York: The Free Press.

25. Goodman-Delahunty, J., Dhami, M.K. and Martschuk, N. (2014) 'Interviewing high value detainees: Securing cooperation and disclosures.' *Applied Cognitive Psychology 28*, 6, 883–897.

26. Start Empathy (2015) 'A toolkit for promoting empathy in schools.' Accessed on 26/6/2017 at https://startempathy.org/resources/toolkit.

27. Durlak, J.A., Weissberg, R.P., Dymnicki, A.B., Taylor, R.D. and Schellinger, K.B. (2011) 'The impact of enhancing students' social and emotional learning: A meta-analysis of school-based universal interventions.' *Child Development 82*, 405–432.

28. L. Buscaglia, Professor of Special Education at the University of Southern California.

CHAPTER TWO

Affective and Cognitive Empathy

The impact of empathy

Empathy is at the heart of relationships. It builds and shapes them. The understanding of the 'other' strengthens bonds and deepens intimacy. And yet empathy has a much more significant role than merely understanding and caring.

> Empathy…is about cultural sensitivity and conflict resolution. It's about the ability to communicate effectively and understand the emotions of others. Empathy is about standing up, not standing by, uncovering what's below the surface through active listening and putting words into action.[1]

Empathy is a vital life skill, and yet empathetic behaviour doesn't 'just happen'. It is 'caught' within a loving and nurturing environment. When these vital elements are missing, empathy will struggle to take hold and develop. Like a seed needs warmth and water to germinate and grow, empathy needs connection.

In an ideal world, every family would provide this loving and nurturing environment, both before and after the birth of a child. However, there are many thousands of families in the UK that live in highly stressful environments due to poverty, abuse, drugs and poor housing. Such environments create different levels of trauma, all resulting in the production of the stress hormone, cortisol. Cortisol is part of our natural defence system, helping to save us when we are at risk. However, in large and constant doses, it slowly strips the brain of vital connections, causing havoc to a growing brain. The ability to learn is critically affected and so too is the ability to connect. Decades of evidence from orphanages in Romania and Albania confirm this.

In the UK, by the time children reach the age of three, a mere thousand days after they are born, 'there are large and systemic differences between children from lower and higher income families and these gaps persist throughout childhood, as later attainment tends to be heavily influenced by early development.'[2] The stress hormone has already started its deadly work.

In the UK, the government has no data on the number of children living in stressful conditions. However, we do know that one in four children in the UK are brought up in poverty. The disadvantages of poverty are profound. Not only do warmth and food elude many such children but a large percentage also misses out on achieving at school, and earning good salaries when they grow up. Children from impoverished backgrounds achieve GCSE grades that are typically 28 per cent lower than the rest of society. They become victims of overdoses of cortisol that change the architecture of their brain, rendering them casualties in the worlds of education and employment.

The good news is that the effects of a warm and loving environment at preschool, teamed with dedicated staff and profound learning experiences can decrease levels of cortisol and create long-term beneficial effects. The key factor in this is the connection between adults and child.

No teacher, anywhere, at any time, will have a greater effect than you, the child's key person in preschool. These vital years of learning shape the brain activity and chemistry that will form the child's future skillsets. This is some responsibility! I believe that it is through empathy, and empathy alone, that we truly reach our key children, and begin to see them fully.

With this in mind, let us start the ball rolling by examining the two different types of empathy and their effect on early years settings.

Affective and cognitive empathy

Empathy is twofold. We *feel emotions* and we *identify emotions.*
Feeling emotions is called *affective empathy.* Our friend
shows up in tears over her relationship. We feel sad. It isn't our
sadness, but we feel it anyway.

We enter the local corner shop and a group of people are
laughing hysterically. We feel a smile tugging at the corners of
our mouth.

We go and see a film that reduces us to tears along with
the rest of the audience. Ten minutes later the sad feeling may
be finished and done with and it's possible that we can't even
remember the name of the protagonist in the film. Affective
empathy may not always be profound or significant, but it will
be *felt.*

Whenever there are other people about, or a connection
with someone, you'll experience affective empathy. You just
can't help yourself. Some of us have stronger affective empathy
than others. We'll come to that later.

Cognitive empathy is when we work out what a person is
feeling and then we try to understand it. In short, *we identify an
emotion.* This is a skill and we *learn* it. For example, our child
comes home from school thrilled to bits to be chosen as the
back end of the donkey in the nativity play. It wouldn't exactly
thrill us in the same way, but we understand her jubilation.
We've identified with her emotion and we know why she
is happy.

Affective and cognitive empathy are found in most people.
However, some people are either deficient in one or the other.
Psychopaths, narcissists and those suffering from schizophrenia
have a deficit in affective empathy. People with autism or
bipolar disorder usually have some sort of impairment with
cognitive empathy.

Both affective and cognitive empathy need to work together
to create a truly empathetic person. But first we need to look at
emotional contagion and understand the role it plays in affecting
our empathy potential.

Emotional contagion

Some of us are more susceptible to affective empathy than others. This is down to *emotional contagion*. Emotional contagion is when we 'catch' someone else's feelings or mood. We become part of someone else's emotional landscape.

> Emotional contagion happens within milliseconds, so quick you can't control it, and so subtly that you're not really aware it's going on. It's critical that people understand emotional contagion is not just a self-contained phenomenon that ends with the 'catching' of the emotions. This contagion influences our cognitions and behaviour – and we often don't even realize the process is happening.[3]

Being highly susceptible to emotional contagion is exhausting. Some of us feel vaguely low and unsettled simply because we have come into contact with someone who is feeling low and unsettled. At the time we don't realise how much it affects us. It is easy to carry on with these negative feelings *that belong to someone else.*

This 'catching' of emotions can be continuous and relentless. If we have no 'filter' or means of understanding the effects of emotional contagion, then we are queuing up for an emotional roller coaster ride. It is vital to have the ability to sieve out the negative vibes that come our way.

How does emotional contagion work? It can take place between two people or among a number of people. First of all there is the 'mimicry' of the emotion shown by the other person. This is automatic. If a child sees another child cry, she might grimace in a similar way. Then comes the feeling. This is sensing a 'pale reflection'[4] of the emotion felt by the other person/people. The result is that we 'catch' the feeling.

Emotional contagion affects *all* human relationships. Strangely, it is the negative emotions that are more infectious than the positive ones. This seems to be an evolutionary instinct because negative emotions are usually linked to our survival.

Emotional contagion can be rife in a school or early years setting. It is a good idea to determine just how susceptible you are to 'catching' another person's mood. You may find yourself going to work each morning only to become unreasonably stressed as you walk through the door. This may have everything to do with emotional contagion, and nothing to do with your present mood.

Try out the Emotional Contagion Scale[5] (see Tables 2.1 and 2.2) to discover how predisposed and susceptible you are to emotional contagion. There are no right or wrong answers. You simply read each question and answer it using the most applicable response for you, using the scale of 1–5. The higher the total, the more predisposed you are to emotional contagion. If your score is 40 or more, you are highly susceptible.

Table 2.1 Emotional contagion scale

		5: Always true for me	4: Often true for me	3: Usually true for me	2: Rarely true for me	1: Never true for me
1	It doesn't bother me to be around angry people					
2	I find myself nodding off when I talk to someone who is depressed					
3	I feel tender and gentle when I see a mother and child hugging each other affectionately					
4	Being around depressed people makes me depressed					
5	I pay attention to what other people are feeling					
6	I feel alive and vibrant when I am with the one I love					

		5: Always true for me	4: Often true for me	3: Usually true for me	2: Rarely true for me	1: Never true for me
7	When someone laughs, I laugh too					
8	When someone hugs me affectionately, I get upset and want to back away					
9	I'm very accurate in judging other people's feelings					
10	When I am around people who are angry, I feel angry myself					
11	I find myself clenching my fist when overhearing others quarrel					
12	I wince when observing someone flinching while getting an injection					
13	I am very sensitive in picking up other people's feelings					
14	I keep a straight face when those around me are laughing hard					
15	Listening to the shrill screams of a terrified child in a dentist waiting room makes me feel nervous					
16	Even if someone I am talking with begins to cry, I don't get teary-eyed					
17	When someone paces back and forth, I feel nervous and anxious					
18	When someone smiles warmly at me, I smile back and feel happy inside					

How did you do? It is important to stress again that there are no right or wrong answers here. You are who you are! However, once we know how susceptible we are to emotional contagion, we can start to filter out some negative or toxic feelings. They aren't ours. We don't want them!

What can you do to reduce emotional contagion in your classroom?

- Pay close attention to your feelings. Notice how different places and different people affect you. You'll see that some people cheer you up, and others bring you down or drain you.

- Look out for sudden changes in your mood, rather than a mood that has been around for some time. Sudden mood swings can be due to contagion as opposed to long-term moods, which are more likely due to our own circumstances or a medical/clinical condition.

- Filter out the negative emotions around you. Positive feelings aren't the problem. Enjoy those! It is the negative ones that need to be alleviated or reduced. We can start to override these negative emotions when we realise that they don't belong to us.

If our environment has the propensity to determine how we feel, then we must create an environment that is upbeat and positive. When the children arrive at the setting in the morning, they need to enter an atmosphere that feels positive and happy. The tone of an environment can determine the behaviour of those who enter it. ER nurses, for example, can calm frightened patients by speaking calmly. As practitioners, we too can focus on bringing a positive emotional contagion to our setting. In this way we can shape the setting's mood.

Incidentally, a positive or cheerful mood makes us more creative while a negative or adverse mood narrows our creativity.

Creativity and children go hand in hand. How appalling if our very moods themselves prevented children from being creative and resourceful!

Emotional contagion in children

Emotional contagion is unregulated in young children. This is because their cognitive abilities haven't yet started to develop properly. They are emotional beings, without the skill to think and reason. As a result, very young children have no 'emotion filters'. However, this early emotional contagion can be a source for good.

Young children will unconsciously mimic and synchronise what someone else is expressing, thereby catching the emotion.[6] Watch children as they play with each other. See how their faces change as they 'see' the emotions of another child. Notice how their voices or movements change. It is entirely automatic.

It is our job to help them to regulate their emotional contagion. They won't be aware that they might be picking up emotional cues or nuances. They won't understand why their feelings might be more powerful at the setting than they are at home.

Children who are particularly susceptible might experience an uncomfortably high level of emotions.

What can you do?

- Be contagious with your optimism and positive approach. Encourage laughter and 'fun' activities. Research on humour indicates that dopamine (the 'happy hormone') is released when we laugh. Laughter and positive emotions are connected. Listen to how much laughter you can hear around you at the setting. Count how often you hear laughter within fifteen minutes. Count how often *you* laugh!

- Notice the child's non-verbal cues. Suggest what she might be feeling: 'We feel sad when someone is crying.' Offer and find solutions together: 'Shall we find your favourite car? Do you know where it is?'

Cognitive empathy

Expressing care for another is not an innate ability present more naturally in some people than others, but rather a skill that can be taught and nurtured through a supportive educational environment.[7]

Being able to understand and 'read' someone is a learned skill. There is a misconception that this will happen automatically. It won't. Cognitive empathy grows due to *brain development* and *experience*. We learn it.

Young children's empathy starts off as 'feelings based' behaviour, where the child has an urge to 'help' based on a feeling. For example, a child might see you drop something on the floor, see you 'upset' and try to give you a kiss or a hug. She isn't quite sure what is going on, but she wants things back to normal. The child can't empathise with you because she has not yet developed *theory of mind*. The development of theory of mind will change everything. This is when a child realises that what she thinks and feels is not the same as everyone else. We will be returning to this in Chapter 3. For now, it is important to realise that *before children develop theory of mind they inhabit a world where they believe other people think and feel as they do*.

Hence there are the tantrums that surge at the age of two. A typical trigger is sharing, a constant challenge for toddlers and young preschoolers. We ask this age group to 'share nicely' when their brains simply cannot yet operate such a cognitive function. Expecting a child to share a toy or understand another child's distress in sharing is rather like asking them to write a book or play a tennis final at Wimbledon. Impossible!

However, once a child has developed theory of mind, she finds herself in a completely different emotional landscape. This is an extremely important 'window of learning' for the child, usually taking place from about the age of three, with some more fundamental changes at the age of four. The child begins to interpret what someone else might be thinking. There is some understanding of why other people behave in such a way. She gradually sees that *other people think and feel differently to her*. It is a complex and sensitive time for young learners.

At this stage of their development we see a change in a child's behaviour from 'feeling based' as shown above, to 'action based'. This is when children are able to offer some kind of tangible help to someone who needs it, related to what they recognise as help. For example, a child might offer a cuddly teddy to someone who is missing her mother, or gently pat her back. She understands that someone is feeling pain, even though *she is not*.

With adult support, children at this stage of their development can learn to recognise and manage their feelings. In direct parallel, children learn to recognise and accept other people's feelings as well.

And here we have the roots of empathy.

Our job as early years practitioners is to ensure that this window of learning is kept wide open. Cognitive empathy will grow in a culture of cognitive empathy! But how can we strengthen this process? How can we make sure that our setting is supporting each and every child in such vital development?

Creating a culture of cognitive empathy
Mind-mindedness

Developing empathy is a simple process. Part of this process is for adults to be empathetic around children. However, children get a significant head start to the empathetic learning process if their parents are aware of mind-mindedness. This is when parents 'tune in' to what their babies are thinking or feeling. Mind-mindedness has a powerful impact on the baby's future ability to understand their own and other people's feelings.

This is powerful. Parents can literally change their child's brain chemistry by talking about the child's thoughts and feelings: 'Look how happy you are to see Teddy!'

By 'reading' the baby's mind, parents appear to start firing up the connections in the brain that are associated with emotional intelligence, the forerunner to empathy.[8]

This type of talk facilitates very early emotional learning. Early years practitioners can use a similar type of dialogue, called *emotional and mental state talk*. This mirrors mind-mindedness, where we tune into what a child is thinking and feeling, and then invite them to talk about it.

Emotional and mental state talk

Children learn to be *cognitively* empathetic when we talk with them about their feelings and when we talk about other people's feelings. There is a direct correlation between such talk and future emotional intelligence. It is thought that the language used (happy, sad, cross, bored, annoyed, lonely, etc.) fires up connections in the brain, and actually grows the grey matter located in parts of the brain. All similar research points to the fact that positive feelings and language are linked with emotional balance and happiness.

Emotional and mental state talk can be divided into three parts: talk which refers to our *desires*, our *feelings*, and our *thinking*.

Talk referring to *desires* is easy to recognise in the toddler. 'I want it!' is a familiar cry. This becomes less frequent when the child reaches three or beyond. Somewhere around this age, the child realises that other people have different desires from her (theory of mind). By the time the child is five or six, these 'I want' expressions are becoming much less frequent.

Two-years-olds start to talk about *feelings*; they might say that their toy is happy or sad. This becomes more complex as they get older, so that between the age of three and five, these feelings can include terms like 'bored' or 'lonely'. Talk about *thinking* comes last of all. Somewhere along the learning process, children start to use thought processes to work things out. This is where children will use phrases like 'I think' or 'I remember'. Language is key in this development. Children whose language is delayed find this thinking state the hardest of all. When adults ask them, 'What do *you* think?' or 'Do you remember...?' they are unable to use language to continue the thought process. This is why sign language is so vital because the thinking process can develop, with or without verbal language. It is interesting to note that deaf children with deaf parents develop this 'thinking talk' skill, because there is an alternative way of 'thinking' language in the way they sign to each other.

It is the constant repetition and consistency of this type of talk that fires up the relevant synapses of the brain. *Talking about desires, feelings and thoughts is the vital backdrop to empathetic behaviour.* Emotional and mental state talk digs deep into what is going on in a child's head and heart. We need to consider that children's actions are almost never due to bad behaviour or naughtiness. They are more likely due to an overpowering urge to take, push, have or claim. We are the support system for that type of behaviour. Emotional and mental state talk is the tool that we can use to help children to understand their own feelings and actions, and those of others.

Self-esteem

The most basic task for one's mental, emotional and social health, which begins in infancy and continues until one dies, is the construction of his/her positive self-esteem.[9]

Our mental, emotional and social health can all be damaged by isolation. We are hardwired for connection right from birth and it is through these connections that our self-esteem grows. Self-esteem is based on the positive and negative self-perceptions we develop over time. We recognise our own worth. We work out who we are and where we fit in.

At roughly the age of 18 months a toddler will recognise herself as a separate person from other people. (You can actually test this by putting a dot on their nose, looking in a mirror with them, and seeing if she touches the dot on her own nose. If she does, she has this 'self-recognition'!)

When a child seems isolated in a setting, this has an impact on her development. Of course, different children have different temperaments. Some are withdrawn and others are approachable. Some are shy while others are confident. Finding a good fit for these children at preschool is absolutely vital for their future happiness and empathy skills. This fit is called 'goodness of fit' and describes compatibility between the child's temperament and the expectations of everyone around them. A shy, withdrawn child will need plenty of encouragement and warmth in order to get used to a new situation while an outgoing, approachable child may find settling in easy.

Our biggest challenge at preschool is to level the playing field when it comes to self-esteem. The two main adult behaviours that are associated with higher child self-esteem are *warmth* and *being democratic*. Warmth can be described as loving and empathetic behaviour. Democratic behaviour is when practitioners allow children to have a voice. Isn't it fascinating that the behaviours that encourage self-esteem are the very same ones that build empathy?

When we model empathy, we build self-esteem. When we listen to children with all of our attention, we build self-esteem. When we talk about feelings, we build self-esteem.

This is a win-win situation.

We build self-esteem, and as a result, we build empathy too.

Awareness of research on skills that precede empathy

Children at preschool are in a critical period of development. *The windows of learning for language, theory of mind, self-understanding and cognitive skills are all wide open.* Each of these 'windows' is connected. The key to keeping these windows wide open is socialising. Socialising requires a variety of skills that can only be gained by *being social*. Practice makes perfect!

There has been a massive surge of research over the last couple of decades; all research demonstrates that empathy grows in a culture of talk, mutual respect and positive responses to each other. Take a look.

The positive side to research

- When children talk about their feelings, and hear you talk about yours, they have stronger social skills.[10]

- When children understand emotions they are more popular with their peers.[11,12]

- Children who talk frequently about their peers (positively) develop stronger preschool social skills.[13]

- When children and adults respond to each other in a sensitive way it promotes social competence.[14]

- Young children's emotional understanding and empathetic response is linked to academic success.[15]

- Young children's emotional understanding and empathetic response is linked to social competence.[16]

- Young children's emotional understanding and empathetic response is linked to better behaviour.[17]

- Emotional well-being (the absence of internalising problems) strongly predicts happiness in adulthood.[18]

- Children who are accepted by their peers tend to be protected against behavioural and emotional problems later on in their school life and beyond.[19]

The negative side to research

- Socially withdrawn children are at risk of depression, linked to insecure attachment relationships with parents.[20]

- Negative emotions (especially from mothers) means that children are less likely to see their parents as people who can comfort or advise them.[21]

- Teachers and parents rate children who play in more 'negative' groups of peers as less socially competent.[22]

- Children who are rejected by their peers when they are very young show higher rates of antisocial behaviour four years later.[23]

Conclusion

Affective *and* cognitive empathy can be strengthened in an empathetic environment. We know that empathy literally 'grows' in the brain. We also know that the capacity for empathy will be lost if those regions of the brain are not used enough. Empathy is *our responsibility* to grow and maintain. We need to establish and reinforce appropriately high expectations. This will help children to develop resilience in both their emotions and behaviour. Early intervention with troubled preschoolers can prevent these young souls from becoming violent teens and adults. All of this happens on our watch!

Notes

1. Ashoka Changemakers (2012) Activating Empathy in Children. Accessed on 11/08/2017 at www.changemakers.com
2. Field, F. (2010) *The Foundation Years: Preventing Poor Children Becoming Poor Adults*. London: Cabinet Office, Whitehall. Accessed on 26/06/2017 at http://webarchive.nationalarchives.gov.uk/20110120090128/http:/povertyreview.independent.gov.uk/media/20254/poverty-report.pdf.
3. Dr. Elaine Hatfield, University of Hawaii. Quoted in Goleman, D. (1991) 'Happy or sad, a mood can prove contagious.' *The New York Times*, 15 October.
4. Hatfield, E., Rapson, R.L. and Le, Y.L. (2009) 'Primitive Emotional Contagion: Recent Research.' In J. Decety and W. Ickes (eds) *The Social Neuroscience of Empathy*. Boston, MA: MIT Press.
5. Doherty, R.W. (1997) 'The emotional contagion scale: a measure of individual differences.' *Journal of Nonverbal Behavior 21*, 2, 131–154. Used by kind permission of Elaine Hatfield.
6. Hatfield, E., Rapson, R.L. and Le, Y. L. (2009) 'Emotional Contagion and Empathy.' In J. Decety and W. Ickes (eds) *The Social Neuroscience of Empathy*. Boston, MA: MIT Press.
7. McLennan, D.M.P. (2008) 'The benefits of using socio-drama in the elementary classroom: Promoting caring relationships among educators and students.' *Early Childhood Education Journal 35*, 5, p.456. Used by kind permission of Deanna McLennan.
8. Meins, E., Muñoz Centifanti, L.C., Fernyhough, C. and Fishburn, S. (2013) 'Maternal mind-mindedness and children's behavioural difficulties: Mitigating the impact of low socioeconomic status.' *Journal of Abnormal Child Psychology 41*, 4, 543–553.
9. Macdonald, G. (1994) 'Self Esteem and the Promotion of Mental Health.' In D. Trent and C. Reed (eds) *Promotion of Mental Health, Vol 3*. Aldershot: Avebury, pp.19–20.
10. Denham, S.A., Mitchell-Copeland, J., Strandberg, K., Auerbach, S. and Blair, K. (1997) 'Parental Contributions to Preschoolers' Emotional Competence: Direct and Indirect Effects.' *Plenum Publishing Corporation 21*, 1, 65–86.
11. Denham, A., McKinley, M., Couchoud, E.A. and Holt, R. (1990) *Emotional and Behavioural Predictors of Preschool Peer Ratings*. Hoboken: Blackwell Publishing Ltd.
12. McDowell, D.J., O'Neil, R. and Parke, R.D. (2000) 'Display rule application in a disappointing situation and children's emotional reactivity relations with social competence.' *Merrill-Palmer Quarterly 46*, 2, 306–324.
13. Laird, R.D., Petit, G.S., Mize, J., Brown, E.G. and Lindsay, E.J. (1994) 'Parent-child conversations about peer relationships: Contributions to competence.' *Family Relations 43*, 425–432.
14. Harrist, A.W., Pettit, G.S., Dodge, K.A. and Bates, J.E. (1994) 'Dyadic synchrony in mother-child interaction: Relation with children's subsequent kindergarten adjustment.' *Family Relations 43*, 417–424.

15. Denham, S.A., Bassett, H. H., Way, E., Mincic, M., Zinsser, K. and Graling, K. (2012) 'Preschoolers' emotion knowledge: Self-regulatory foundations, and predictions of early school success.' *Cognition & Emotion 26*, 4, 667–679.

16. Denham, S.A. *et al.* (2003) 'Preschool emotional competence pathway to social competence?' *Child Development 74*, 238–256.

17. Denham, S.A. *et al.* (2002) 'Preschool understanding of emotions: Contributions to classroom anger and aggression.' *Journal of Child Psychology and Psychiatry 43*, 7, 901–916.

18. Furnham, A. and Cheng, H. (2000) 'Perceived parental behaviour, self-esteem and happiness.' *Social Psychiatry and Psychiatric Epidemiology 35*, 10, 463–470.

19. Criss, M.M., Pettit, G.S., Bates, J.E., Dodge, K.A. and Lapp, A.L. (2002) 'Family adversity, positive peer relationships, and children's externalising behavior: A longitudinal perspective on risk and resilience.' *Child Development 73*, 1220–1237.

20. Gullone, E., King, N.J. and Ollendick, T.H. (2006) 'The role of attachment representation in the relationship between depressive symptomatology and social withdrawal in middle childhood.' *Journal of Child and Family Studies 15*, 3, 271–285.

21. Denham *et al.* (1997).

22. Denham, S. *et al.* (2001) 'Preshoolers at play: Co-socialisers of emotion and social competence.' *International Journal of Behavioral Development 25*, 290–301.

23. Dodge, K.A. *et al.* (2003) 'Peer rejection and social information-processing factors in the development of aggressive behavior problems in children.' *Child Development 74*, 374–393.

CHAPTER THREE

Empathy and Theory of Mind

Jackie Harland

Theory of mind is foundational to empathy, our ability to put ourselves in 'someone else's shoes'. It is the bedrock of our social understanding. While empathy involves an emotional response to another person's mental state, theory of mind is a more complex cognitive ability, a crucial component of which is *understanding someone else's perspective.*

Joel and Sam are fighting over a blue toy car. Their mother separates them and tells Sam that it is Joel's turn with the car. Sam walks away, cross and upset. A short while, later Joel hides the blue car in a cupboard and goes to the toilet. Sam is watching. While Joel is out of the room he takes the car from the cupboard and puts it under a cushion that he subsequently sits on.

Where does Joel go to get his car when he comes back? To the cupboard or the cushion? He goes to the cupboard. We know this because we understand Joel's 'knowledge' (or lack of it in this case) and therefore his subsequent behaviour. This understanding is called theory of mind.

Theory of mind helps us to realise that others not only feel and think differently to us, but also that they have knowledge and beliefs that differ from ours. Children as young as eighteen months will assume an adult likes and dislikes the same food as they do. As a result, when presented with two different bowls of food, the child will feed the adult with the option that they themselves prefer. This assumption that others have the same thoughts, feelings and opinions changes as theory of mind develops. Theory of mind allows us to work out how someone may be feeling and what he believes or intends. We can start to predict what that person might do because we understand his perspective.

When I was working with a 12-year-old girl with autism and an underdeveloped theory of mind, I decided to make a chart showing her and my favourite food in order to illustrate our different perspectives. Everything was going well as we discussed how much she liked crisps, biscuits and cheese. However, when I wrote on the chart that I liked scrambled eggs she became extremely upset, shouting 'No, no!' To her, scrambled eggs were disgusting. Her difficulty in seeing the perspective of others had had a significant impact on her behaviour at school. For example, she would laugh if she saw someone hurt and crying, and would make comments such as 'That's a funny face.' She had limited theory of mind.

Lacking theory of mind means that life is unpredictable and alarming. We have no 'tool' to predict or second-guess what other people may do.

The development of theory of mind

Theory of mind gradually develops throughout the early years, and is continually 'refined' throughout school and into adulthood.

Precursors to theory of mind emerge at a preverbal stage with the development of joint attention between a parent and a child. Joint attention involves reciprocal responses, which describes the shared interaction between a child and another person. Joint attention allows young children to recognise and respond to facial expressions. Joint attention includes vital shared attention on an object of interest, and it encourages engagement and involvement. It encompasses the emotional awareness of another's feelings. In other words, it is the early stages of empathy.

Muris *et al.* (1999)[1] recognised that the process continues with children accepting that other people have needs, emotions and mental states. For example, they realise that when someone loses their dog, they would be sad. They begin to use words such as 'know', 'think', 'remember'. Language is essential for theory of mind as without language there is no 'theory'. Early development of theory of mind can use visual imagery but more complex aspects of theory of mind require language based thought.

Children's social interactions with peers and adults trigger the development of theory of mind. This is habitually through play at around three to four years of age. Children begin to understand that their mind can represent things that are not immediately present and they begin to act out scenarios in pretend play. In other words, they can think about a person, situation or object, and can understand not only how he is feeling, but also how that feeling will affect his behaviour: 'He is crying because he is sad and he misses his mummy.' This understanding of *cause and effect* with emotions is another important precursor to theory of mind. Children learn to predict how someone might feel in a situation: 'He will be sad if he loses his teddy.'

Furthermore, the crucial revelation that someone may have a different belief and that this belief will affect his behaviour, emerges in children at around four to five years of age. This is a critical stage in social relationships and in how children play. Children are now able to think about 'others' rather than 'self'. It alters how they perceive others, and is the starting point of empathetic behaviour.

Finally, an essential feature of theory of mind that depends on 'emotional cognition' is false belief understanding. This is the concept of belief versus reality, desire and pretence. It allows a child to understand humour, sarcasm and tricking. This skill can emerge at around five to six years of age.

The development of theory of mind has huge significance for the child's communication, behaviour and connection with others. It will affect how he negotiates, plays and interacts. An important influence here is the child's development of pragmatic skills, his ability to use language appropriately in context and to take into consideration his listener's knowledge and interest. As these skills become more secure, theory of mind will have an increasing effect on a child's judgements, trust of others and social behaviour. In short, it is the vital precursor to empathy. Empathy cannot exist without it.

Testing theory of mind

Simon Baron-Cohen, director of the Autism Research Centre at Cambridge University, speaks of 'mindblindness', where children with delay in the development of theory of mind are 'blind' to the workings of another's thoughts or feelings. As a result, these children will find other people's behaviour potentially unpredictable, baffling and perhaps alarming, such as the girl in the scrambled egg story above.

Baron-Cohen, Leslie and Frith (1985)[2] were keen to examine the development of theory of mind in four-year-olds, and adapted an experiment previously carried out by two developmental psychologists, Heinz Wimmer and Josef Perner. This became known as the Sally-Anne Test. The experiment involved 61 children, 20 of whom had a diagnosis of autism, 14 who had Down's syndrome and 27 who were described as 'clinically unimpaired'.

The children were shown two dolls, one called Sally and one called Anne. Sally had a basket and Anne had a box. Sally placed a marble in her basket, covered the basket and walked away. While Sally was gone, Anne took the marble out of the basket and placed it in her box. Sally was brought back and the children were asked a belief question, 'Where will Sally look for the marble?'

In order to pass the test the child needed to say that Sally would look in her basket, showing that he recognises her lack of knowledge and understands her perspective.

If the child was unable to see another's perspective he would answer that Sally will look in the box. He *assumes* that Sally's knowledge is the same as his. A reality question could then be asked to those who 'passed' the test: 'Where is the marble really?'

Cohen and Frith found that:

- 23 out of the 27 'unimpaired' four-year-olds passed this test (85%)

- 12 out of 14 children with Down's syndrome passed (86%)

- 5 out of 20 children with autism passed (25%).

Although this experiment shows interesting findings, its assumptions for children with autism have been questioned. This is because other factors, such as understanding of the language involved, could impact their response. It is important not to see this as a diagnostic tool for children at risk of autism but something that, along with other false belief tests, can give vital information on a child's development of theory of mind.

Simple theory of mind test to use at preschool

The Smartie Box Test[3] is easily administered in a preschool setting.

Child A is presented with a Smartie box and when he opens it he finds it is filled with pencils, not Smarties. The adult closes the box and asks Child A this question: 'If I call over Child B and give them the Smartie box, what will they think is in the box?'

A three–year-old who has not yet developed theory of mind is likely to answer 'pencils'. This is because he believes everyone sees the world as he does. However, a four-year-old whose theory of mind is emerging may well understand that Child B has not yet discovered that there are no actual Smarties in this box. As a result, he will say 'Smarties'.

Why is theory of mind so important?

Theory of mind is the aspect of our social cognition that differentiates us exclusively from other primates. Theory of mind has many benefits that influence our behaviour and our social attitude:

- It enables us to 'mind read', anticipating someone's behaviour and feelings.

- It allows us to respond with sensitivity.

- It helps us to be responsive, recognising when communication is 'cross' or 'unhappy' and adapting our speech and behaviour accordingly.

- It helps us to agree/disagree with people, supporting them in a relevant and loving manner.

- It allows us to empathise with others.

- It helps us to persuade someone to think differently.

- It supports our ability to teach and inform.

- It enables us to trick and deceive, as the ability to change someone else's belief system is activated.

Children with poor theory of mind will 'assume' our knowledge and start talking about people or situations without introducing or explaining them to us. Consequently we will have no idea of what they are talking about and repeatedly have to ask questions. *Such deficits of theory of mind have a significant impact on a child's ability to form enjoyable and meaningful relationships and to function successfully in society.*

In early childhood theory of mind is at the heart of play. The ability to get on with others and understand their needs and point of view is extremely important. Three-year-olds begin to talk about what other people think and know. They have a developing awareness that children are happy when they get what they want, and cry when they don't.[4] This emerging responsiveness is important for children's communication skills in sharing interest and commenting on their environment. It enables children to learn to resolve conflicts, empathise with friends and share successes. Conversely, a child with a strong theory of mind can also use this negatively to manipulate and control others.

As children develop and rely more on verbal communication to make and maintain relationships, theory of mind plays a significant role not only in friendships but also in academic success. In academic areas theory of mind encourages more complex play, problem solving, reasoning and the ability to make inferences and predict. These higher order language skills become increasingly important as children progress through school.

Astington and Edward[5] describe theory of mind as a 'system with biological roots' that develops without having to be specifically taught. They believe that theory of mind develops rather like language, caught from the interactions and environment of the child. Vitally, though, they recognise that the child's environment will boost or hinder the development of theory of mind.

How to develop theory of mind

Children learn how to consider the feelings, thoughts and beliefs of others by looking beyond their own feelings, thoughts and beliefs.

The social environment influences the development of theory of mind. Children gradually construct social understanding through their interactions with others in the real world. Language and interaction are the starting posts in creating the 'mental world' of the child, where children learn how to think and what to believe. Through language they discover that others think and believe differently. They 'go beyond their own private thoughts and beliefs to consider the thoughts and beliefs of others'.[6]

Language, then, is the bedrock, the base from which theory of mind can spring. However, there are other important factors that we can plant in the preschool setting that will encourage further the development of theory of mind.

Pretend play

Play is the highest form of research.[7]

Play is an essential component of a child's holistic development. Pretend play, creating a narrative or scenario and assigning identities or roles, will significantly support the development of theory of mind. Early make-believe play can emerge as early as eighteen months where children will substitute imaginary situations for real ones. Pretend play is one of the areas of development that is commonly impaired in children with autism.

Giving children opportunities and resources to encourage elaborate pretend and cooperative play will support their development of theory of mind. Foundational to pretend play is the symbolic and representational nature of objects and toys. For example, a child pretends a cardboard box is a truck because their thoughts are different from reality, and he is indulging his imagination. In pretend play children employ a number of social skills. He observes and responds to the behaviour and choices of others, he deals with conflict and he recognises the likes and dislikes of peers. Parents can encourage role-play as this encourages children to think from someone else's perspective.

Pretend play can be encouraged by:

- following the child's interest/s

- modelling the role-play alongside the child

- providing a mixture of real objects and toys (use toys that are similar to the 'real' object, e.g. a stick for a thermometer)

- acting out favourite stories, for example, *We're Going on a Bear Hunt*.

Reading imaginative stories

Reading imaginative stories will trigger theory of mind especially those that involve surprises, pretending and tricking. This helps the child to understand that someone's belief may not reflect reality. For example, the wicked queen in Snow White pretends to be an old lady to get Snow White to take the apple. The wolf dresses up as granny to trick Little Red Riding Hood. Stories can build social understanding of situations, show people's responses and behaviours, and give the children opportunities to guess what might happen next.

Use of specific vocabulary and language

Using phrases such as 'I think...' and 'I feel...' will also be helpful. It is essential to put into words what you are thinking and feeling to support the child's social understanding. Explaining to children why people behave as they do in different situations is important in developing theory of mind and will demonstrate cause and effect, for example, 'James is feeling sad because he has lost his favourite car.' Telling simple jokes and using figurative language will also support their understanding that we can say things that are not necessarily true. For example, 'It is raining cats and dogs.'

Mindfulness

Astington and Edward[8] talk about factors in a child's social environment that will support their development of theory of mind. Mothers who talk about how they are feeling, what they are thinking and what they like or love are supporting such development. Parental and teacher conversational elaboration will impact a child's development of social understanding and theory of mind. Teachers can highlight how they or the children may be feeling in certain situations and thereby build understanding of emotions and feelings: 'Sarah is sad because her new coat has mud on it.'

Talking about events

> *Talking about events in personal life history helps children to understand how knowledge, in this case, memory of those events, comes about.*[9]

Children need to develop their knowledge and understanding of events. With this comes a growing understanding of people's behaviours and feelings. Together these create an 'emotional source' for developing theory of mind. Memory of events plays an essential role in this. Talking about a significant birthday party encourages a child to observe, reflect and remember. It reminds children about how they felt and how others responded, for example, 'Do you remember how everyone shouted when the big birthday cake was brought into the room?'

A practitioner can help to build memories by encouraging children to bring photos or souvenirs of events into preschool, helping them to retell the event with questions to scaffold the narrative, for example, 'Who came to your party?' 'Tell me about the sparkly candles on your cake.' This may also include higher order thinking such as inference. To make an inference regarding someone else's perspective the child must combine their observations with stored knowledge to come up with an idea. For example, asking, 'Do you think your sister liked her birthday cake?' will help the child to consider memories of their sister's response and combine this with the knowledge of how children generally like cakes. Talking about events together will build that knowledge and understanding and asking the child relevant questions will stimulate new ideas and foster new ways of thinking.

Social Stories™

Difficulty in understanding someone else's perspective can cause children to feel extremely vulnerable and lead to conflicts and isolation. Resources developed by Carol Gray[10] have been found to support children with social communication needs and high functioning autism. These are called Social Stories™. They are based in evidence-based practice and are widely used to develop theory of mind.

A Social Story™ is a social learning strategy, which focuses on developing social understanding. This is important, as it is easy to focus on social behaviour that can be limiting for the child. For example, we tell a child with autism that it is always important to make eye contact. The child may take this literally, which is clearly not appropriate in some situations.

The 'author' of a Social Story™ develops the story on behalf of the child. He gathers information and then writes a personalised text with some illustrations. This serves to support the child's social understanding of a particular social context, skill, achievement or concept. All stories need to be descriptive, meaningful and safe for the child. The following is an example of a Social Story™.

LINING UP

Every day in my classroom we line up to go outside. I like being first in line. My teacher says who will be first each day. When I am first I have lots of space and my friends don't touch me.

My friends like being first too. They like space as well. They don't mean to touch me; sometimes they just need to move.

My teacher has a list so we can all have a turn. That is fair so my friends can be first when it is their turn. I can wait, as soon it will be my turn again.

A Social Story™ outlines the steps or stages of a social context and brings new understanding of any expectations of behaviour or attitude. In other words, it brings perspective to a situation.

This powerful process works best when shared with the child on a regular basis, providing crucial support for those children who struggle to cope in certain social contexts.

Conclusion

Children need to use theory of mind in just about every interaction they have in a social setting. It is necessary to engage, to understand, to share interest and to learn. Theory of mind enables children to develop and maintain meaningful friendships and to successfully participate in cooperative and pretend play. Without the ability to understand and anticipate what others might be feeling or what they may do, a child will feel extremely vulnerable in both his social settings and in terms of his learning.

Children who learn to understand other people's beliefs, needs and intentions, through the natural development of theory of mind, will become more empathetic. By encouraging and supporting this crucial development in the preschool classroom, we begin the groundwork for empathy, on which the child's social and emotional health is built.

The development of theory of mind is often not considered in early years settings. This allows for a gap in the understanding of why young children behave as they do. If we have children with weak theory of mind, we will notice a difference in behaviour and performance. They will find it difficult to participate, cooperate or contribute to their immediate community.

Theory of mind is easily tested and with understanding can be supported and developed, carrying children successfully through social relationships and learning. Testing our children for theory of mind is essential. These tests allow us to see where they 'are' and where they need to go, which is the foundation of empathetic teaching. Professionals, armed with understanding and knowledge, can be supportive of any children with weak theory of mind, working to develop the vital theory of mind skills and the coexisting emerging empathy. This will navigate those children through the challenges of social relationships and learning, resulting in increased well-being and emotional health.

Notes

1. Muris, P., Steerneman, P., Meesters, C., et al. (1999) 'The TOM Test: A new instrument for assessing theory of mind in normal children and children with pervasive developmental disorders.' Journal of Autism and Developmental Disorders 29, 1, 67–78.
2. Baron-Cohen, S., Leslie, A.M. and Frith, U. (1985) 'Does the autistic child have "theory of mind"?' Cognition 21, 37–46.
3. Kerner, J., Frith, U., Leslie, A. and Leekam, S.R. (1989) 'Exploration of the Autistic Child's Theory of Mind: Knowledge, Belief and Communication.' Child Development 60, 689–700. Used by permission of Wiley.
4. Wellman, H.M. and Banerjee, M. (1991) 'Mind and emotion: Children's understanding of the emotional consequences of beliefs and desires.' British Journal of Developmental Psychology 9, 2, 191–214.
5. Astington, J. and Edward, M. (2010) The Development of Theory of Mind in Early Childhood. New Brunswick, Canada: Institute of Child Study, University of Toronto.
6. Astington, J. and Baird, J. (2005) Why Language Matters for Theory of Mind. Oxford: Oxford University Press, p.12.
7. Albert Einstein.
8. Astington and Edward (2010).
9. Wang, Z. (2015) 'Theory of mind and children's understanding of teaching and learning during early childhood.' Cogent Education 2, 1.
10. Gray, C. (2017) 'Social Stories™.' Accessed on 26/6/2017 at http://carolgraysocialstories.com/about-2/carol-gray.

CHAPTER FOUR

Establishing Empathy in Our Pedagogy

Pedagogy is the learning 'ecosystem' in which children grow. It is everything that we do and say as we work with them. It is how we greet the children in the morning, how we join in their play, how we interact and relate. It is about what is displayed on the walls, how the equipment is arranged and how the toys are accessed. It is our very attitude to life, mirrored in our teaching.

As practitioners, we are agents of possibility for children, unlocking the door of each child's learning potential with the key of empathy. Children can make choices, and become decision makers in their learning simply because of our approach to it. Conversely, children can be swamped with 'teacher control', and lose their initiative, their power to choose and decide. They can become pawns in the game of learning rather than the key players.

Pestalozzi, a Swiss social reformer and educator, born in 1746, argued that children must follow their own interests, learning by doing and playing. More importantly, he stressed the education of the head, heart and hands, highlighting *how the heart must lead*. Empathy was thus embedded deep into his pedagogy.

Pestalozzi's reforms still resonate with most early childhood pedagogies, and many use his philosophy today. The Early Years Foundation Stage (EYFS, UK), Montessori, Reggio Emilia and Te Whariki are all examples of a child-led curriculum, each with significantly distinctive principles and values.

The EYFS (UK) believes in the unique child. It considers an enabling and empowering environment to be key, and that warm and positive relationships between adult and child are central to the child's learning and development.

Montessori (Italy and Global) believes in a carefully organised environment which allows children to have uninterrupted blocks of time to explore. Children are seen as very capable learners, especially when supported by the right environment, one that fosters their natural desire to learn.

Reggio Emilia (Italy and Global) also sees the child as competent and capable. Teachers and children explore together. The environment is seen as the 'third teacher', providing endless opportunities for exploration and inquiry.

Te Whariki (New Zealand) has a strong sociocultural vision, where relationships between family and community, child and teacher, school and family are woven into the fabric of the curriculum. Empowerment of the child is key, with a holistic view of the child's development.

Each of these pedagogies was born out of a unique need. Reggio Emilia was created after the Second World War, an uprising against Fascism and a determined vision for a child-centred philosophy, leading to social democracy. Maria Montessori was one of the first female doctors of her time and her pedagogy was born out of her scientific observations of children and how they best learn. Te Whariki was built on the shared vision of a strong and united community, based on the partnership between teachers and families.

Pedagogy will either create an environment of empowered learning or, at worst, one of 'benign neglect'. Pedagogy informs every interaction, activity or routine. It is the foundation of our teaching. Getting it right is vital. All too often we bypass pedagogical theories, unaware of their crucial position in a child's learning and well-being. We need to reflect on our pedagogy, always considering and studying what methods work and why. Such reflection is the greatest lever we possess for improving and cultivating children's future success and happiness. We need to get it right!

Best practice pedagogy

The best quality settings use the following child-centred pedagogy:

- high-quality interactions
- listening to the child's voice
- learning through play
- assessment and monitoring that informs the child's provision, and provides support for success in learning.

High quality interactions

Children naturally seek out interaction. Think how many times children invite us to play! This built-in need to connect creates the perfect scenario for powerful learning. Such interactions 'will literally change the chemistry of (a child's) brain by establishing the essential connections needed for the child's future social and emotional skills.'[1]

The following theories on interaction have impacted pedagogies worldwide:

- **Scaffolding:** Scaffolding is the support we offer to a child's play through *talking together, thinking aloud and modelling.* Again, the quality of our interaction is of paramount importance. 'Tailored' scaffolding boosts the potential for powerful play and learning. If we simply offer a sentence starter here and there, or we ask closed questions, we are falling far short of high-quality interaction. When scaffolding is effective, it kick-starts learning like no other method of teaching. Adult and child become fully absorbed in joint, cooperative exploration. They discover together, think together and enjoy the play together.

- **What can you do?** Follow the child's interests and play with them. Use plenty of 'discovery' and 'thinking' language: 'I think we'd better find ...' 'Do you know where...' 'I wonder where...' Joint discovery is exciting for the child. Do plenty of it: 'Let's find some bugs under here...' 'Let's ask Mrs S if she knows...' Enjoy the activity, making your enjoyment visible: 'I love doing this with you.' 'I am having fun, are you?' Joint enjoyment is a catalyst. Children feel valued and loved when they know that you are genuinely involved in their play and that you are genuinely enjoying it; it allows their learning to then take on a new, deeper level of interest.

- **Growth mindset:** Children's well-being is affected by how they view themselves. Preconceptions about how 'bright' they are, or how 'well' they can do can impact mindset either negatively or positively. This is known as a 'fixed' mindset, or a 'growth' mindset. When adults interact with a child, praising them for their *effort*, the potential for a growth mindset can flourish. When children are praised for their own *intelligence or cleverness*, the potential for growth mindset is weakened. Practitioners need to know the difference. Ignorance is not bliss, it is damaging.

  - **What can you do?** Praise the effort the children make, for example: 'I love your picture, you've worked really hard with the trees and the sky'; 'Great running, look how far you ran!'; 'Your model is so strong, you worked really hard at sticking it together.' It is the process we praise, and not the outcome. In this way, the children are continually encouraged in terms of their effort and persistence and not by how clever they are. Cleverness is limited but growth and development are boundless.

- **Modelling:** When practitioners interact by modelling activities or behaviours, the child's natural mimicry copies it. This is powerful learning. The child can embrace a challenge, by watching and mimicking us. We need to keep this carefully tailored to their level. She will quickly tire if the modelling is too arduous.

  - **What can you do?** Take advantage of every activity to model behaviour and expected outcome, keeping your modelling warm, considerate and generous. For example, in the role-play corner: 'Are you making dinner? Shall we lay the table?'; 'Jane's baby is sleeping, do we need to be quiet?' Let children take the lead, modelling expected outcomes as the play progresses: 'We are going to the park with the babies? Shall I bring the buggies?' Model expected behaviour: 'I have to wait, it's not my turn yet.' 'Would you like to share my play dough?'

High-quality interactions build the 'conditions' for playing and learning. We become more adept at such interactions through day-to-day practice and repetition. Children are not the only learners in the classroom!

Listening to the child's voice

All children have a 'voice'. They make decisions and choices, and through these they gradually recognise that they are becoming competent and capable. In this way they become a valued member of the community. Expressing their voice is vital; not only do *they* have something to say, but they can also learn to listen to what *other children* have to say. The setting becomes a communication-rich environment.

All children may have a voice, but not all children are heard. Anxiety and unease can control children's decision-making and so they learn to keep quiet. These children often become passengers in their learning, rather than drivers. A child with 'agency', a child with a voice that is heard, operates with autonomy and is a far more effective learner than one who is not.

The child's voice is their communication tool. Without it she is powerless. And yet 'listening to the child's voice' has a worrying ambiguity. Practitioners set out times to 'listen to the child's voice' and put up displays that 'show the child's voice' and take measures to 'monitor the child's voice'. We can become so consumed by protocol and process that we don't actually *hear* what the child is saying to us over the course of the day. We are at risk of ticking boxes, rather than really listening to the children.

Children become more confident, engaged and cooperative when teachers:[2]

- listen effectively to how children express themselves

- have sensitive interactions with children, understanding their ability to contribute

- act as facilitators, organising but enabling children to take the lead.

How do we listen to the child's voice each day?

- **We allow them to become active participants in what happens 'now and next'** in the day-to-day planning and in the choice of equipment. When children are part of the planning process, they cannot be passive observers. They have agency. We keep these choices small to start with, becoming more open-ended as the children get used to such choice making. Practitioners need to support all decisions, avoiding tokenistic or contrived choice making.

- **We develop the language for choice making.** 'Shall we ride the bikes through the puddles, or go for a rainy walk?' This question contains rich language *and* a choice.

- **We listen, watch and observe fastidiously.** We give the children our full attention, taking an active interest and making our enjoyment visible.

- **We wait while children respond to us**, giving them plenty of time. Children often need time and space to work out what their choice/decision/view of the world is and then to express this.

In all of this we need to consider the following:

- **The child's voice does not always use words.** The 'voice' can be silent, withdrawn or absent. Stress, that enemy of learning, may strip the child of a voice, leaving her vulnerable and powerless. We may need to become the child's voice: 'You have sand in your hair. Let's ask James to stop throwing it. It isn't good to throw sand.' In telling 'James' not to throw sand, involve the child: 'Stephen has sand in his hair. He needs you to stop throwing it, doesn't he, Stephen?' Encourage the child's voice; praise her for the smallest of steps: 'Well done for saying no. Saying no tells people what we like and don't like.'

- **A child's voice can be negative.** We must allow that negative voice to speak. When we actively discourage children in expressing their dislikes, they are only expressing half of what they would like to! Once the negative words are out of their mouth, we can model and scaffold the child in finding more positive attitudes: 'You don't like James? I like James. I like it when he rides his bike outside and he laughs as he goes by!' In this way, the child feels heard, but hears another point of view. She might not agree with the 'other' opinion, but she knows that there is one.

Learning through play

Play is not frivolous. It is not a luxury. It is not something to fit in after completing all the normal stuff. Play is the important stuff. Play is a need, a drive, a brain building must-do.[3]

The urge to play is strong, fixed in our children from birth. This motivation, known as conation, is the inner drive to explore and discover.

Children don't play simply because it is fun or enjoyable. These are the by-products of play. Children play because they are wired to play.[4]

There are many other by-products to play. In the first 260 weeks of their lives, children learn to talk, walk, think, understand and interact. They become cooperative, working out how to regulate their own behaviour. Through playful exploration, children's learning potential is improved, their memory is built and their self-esteem is established. There are no losers in the game of play!

Since children have a natural desire to play, their intrinsic motivation is already in place, along with vital positive dispositions, such as curiosity, persistence and enthusiasm. However, these dispositions will be lacking if a child has experienced significant negativity during the first 260 weeks of their life. What do we do then?

How can we create positive play in our setting? How do we restore positive dispositions?

Create a physical environment that is inviting, engaging and rewarding

The physical environment has the most immediate effect on a child's sense of enjoyment and learning. Recent research in Lucknow, India,[5] showed a dramatic increase in learning once the physical environment had been transformed. Initially the early years classroom for three-year-olds was furnished with desks, a timetable and very limited areas for free play. Children's learning indicated a marked lack in social and emotional learning, but high achievement in mathematics and literacy. The classroom was transformed into a welcoming space, where the children could play, access toys for themselves and make choices for the first time. The children could explore and learn on their own terms. As a result, their learning was transformed. *Social and emotional learning, along with listening skills and understanding all increased significantly within three months.*

Children who are absorbed and intent on their play will learn more. Not only this, but their potential for empathy will be increased. Why? Positive dispositions such as resilience, self-motivation and perseverance are all highly sensitive to an enabling physical environment. In other words, children's dispositions are developed, supported or weakened by the physical environment. The environment can be used to 'grow' positive dispositions and eliminate the negative ones.

Create a social and emotional environment that is warm, safe and trusting

Practitioners set the daily emotional tone of the setting. Nurturing relationships between practitioners and children generate a sense of safety and trust. This in turn supports the child as she develops vital social and emotional skills.

A child is either a willing participant in a thriving ecosystem of warmth and trust, or a victim of an environment that is not a 'good fit' for her temperament, however loving the adults may be.

As practitioners, we need to be meticulous in how we deliver our emotional environment. Research indicates that teacher training is critical in developing such skills. Lack of training and knowledge can cause damage to learning, however well-meaning we are. How can we ensure that social and emotional skills are supported and encouraged?

Nurturing and positive interactions promote brain development. Children need to talk about their problems, their challenges and their joys. Our job is to connect with them, and to actively listen to them. The quality of a child's relationships affects the physical structure of their brain[6] and it is through these positive relationships that children develop persistence, competence and enthusiasm for learning.

Supportive relationships can compensate for early negative relationships. It is possible for children to develop well, despite all sorts of hardships, providing they have the opportunity to build positive and healthy relationships with caring and sensitive adults.

The emotional tone of our setting literally builds the brains of our children, making them more effective and engaged learners. Let's set the right tone!

Create an intellectual environment that is full of encouragement, exploration and inquiry

Research supports the theory that children who engage in high-quality play do better at school, and have superior language, comprehension, attention, concentration, cooperation, collaborative and empathetic skills. This is quite a list!

Our intellectual environment needs to meet the needs of the child and her ever-growing brain. For the older children 'mature' play is vital within the intellectual environment. Mature play is what it says on the tin, when play reaches its more mature level. Children can play to their heart's content, but if such play is more typical of a much younger child's activities, the benefits will be largely absent.

Mature play consists of children imagining, taking on diverse roles, making increasingly complex rules, and developing greater flexibility. Mature play is long-lasting, sometimes spanning days and weeks.

Language is key to this play, as children work out what exactly they are playing, how they will play it, and explain its workings to other children wanting to join in. This language can be complex or simple, but there will always be an element of negotiation, where children discuss the best way to plan the play.

This is where we come in. We need to support the children without becoming too involved or directive. Our genuine interest in the activity is important.

We can have many potential roles as mature play partners:

- We can *support* the child in her play, offering ideas, extending her thinking and giving her as much time as she needs to work out what she wants.

- We can *model* what we wish the child to be or do. For example, if the child wants to know more about a dinosaur, we can model 'asking' another adult for some information.

- We can *listen* very carefully to her, giving our full attention. This is extremely powerful for the child, having an adult hanging on every word, and reflecting her ideas and thoughts back to her.

- We can *plan* with the child. When we see her interest in an area is evident, we can go about planning further interactions together, or create new and different activities that will engage the child and extend that learning.

Children's play can remain stereotyped and dull. When we step in we can extend it, deepen it and help them to transform their play into a richer learning experience. Children may well be the play 'experts' but we are the support system for informing and scaffolding play, and perhaps regenerating tired play, converting it into something truly captivating and riveting.

Create an environment that measures the learning by the activity rather than by the clock

Children need an environment where there is plenty of time to play, and where they have the luxury of developing their emerging ideas in large blocks of time. Ample time is key.

Play is a complicated old business. While it veers from fun to serious, from silly to solemn, it is always engaging. The point of a child's play is to make sense of the world, to make sense of all the people in their world, of the way things work, the way things connect and relate to each other. It is hard work, and it takes time.

Child 'agency' is vital, where the child feels in control of the things around her, and where she feels she can influence those things. While we can act as a support to this play, we should never undermine the child's agency by hijacking it and pursuing our ideas instead of the child's. Neither should we remove children's agency by limiting her time and space to immerse herself in the learning process. We habitually put things away, tidying up, as if that is the goal, and not the learning that took place beforehand!

Allowing time and space to explore supports a child's agency. Children need to be able to examine, consider, delve, ask questions, get things right, get things wrong and learn from their mistakes. This won't happen in a setting where we look at the clock rather than the activity. Clearly, we should be guided by the physical time. However, if we create a mindset that thinks long term, providing as much uninterrupted and continuous play as possible, children will reap the benefits.

Assessment

Assessment has to be meaningful. It informs children's learning. In the same way that a doctor needs to carefully observe patients and prescribe the relevant treatment, practitioners need to carefully observe children and deliver the appropriate planning.

We have an advantage over a doctor. We know the children well. We play and interact with them, building an understanding of them. We know their families and their community. We can build up a three-dimensional, all-round knowledge of the child's personality, temperament and interests.

Empathy is part of assessment because assessment demands connection. When we observe, we need to 'tune in' to the child. Such tuning in is at the heart of empathy. We block out distractions and interruptions. We play with the child until we understand what motivates and interests them. We step into their shoes and see the world through their eyes.

It is at this point that we are ready to deliver tailored and relevant planning,

What is the best method of assessment? How do we best understand the child and support her learning? Meaningful assessment:

1. Takes place in a variety of contexts: inside, outside, individually, in groups, at different times of the day and in different activities.

2. Demonstrates what a child can do, not what she cannot; assessment follows the child's interests, focusing on what is significant and meaningful in her world.

3. Observes the child's dispositions, both positive and negative; considering the process as more significant than the outcome.

4. Emphasizes what a child can do when provided with support and encouragement, rather than only measuring what a child can do unaided.

5. Informs and promotes future learning.[7]

From this list, we can see that the uniqueness of the child is central to assessment and that 'tuning in' (empathy) is knitted into the process. Highly effective assessment means that we really 'see' the child. We consider the child's interests, joys and concerns and we marry this consideration with a sound understanding of holistic child development. Highly effective assessment requires us to get down in the trenches with the children, to support and encourage them through the ups and downs of early childhood – in short, to walk in their shoes and see with their eyes.

Conclusion

Pedagogy is deeply personal. It develops from theories, practice, reflections, experiences and needs. It is often culturally informed – relevant to a particular community or social group. It is based on our knowledge of play, learning, child development, environment and relationships. It influences every classroom and child. We need to clarify the principles of our pedagogy – what it is exactly – if we are to optimise our children's chances of success.

> In clarifying…[pedagogy] we can develop a deeper understanding of what is informing our practice, and importantly why we work in particular ways. This in turn can enable us to make our practice, and the impact of our practice, more visible not only to others but also to ourselves.[8]

A strong, informed pedagogy is a gamechanger because it creates a community of inquiry into what we do and why we do it. It is out of this shared and ongoing reflection that we 'grow' our pedagogy. Pedagogy is crucially built out of communal understanding.

And finally, it is the quality of early interactions that 'wire' the brain. This must be at the very heart of our pedagogy. When we fully understand this, when we consider it as we practise on a daily basis, we plant the child in an emotional ecosystem that encourages and stimulates learning and development, and has long-lasting effects on lifelong physical and mental health.

Notes

1. Garnett, H. (2016) 'Play: Part one.' Accessed on 26/6/2017 at http://wonderfulmama.com.
2. Laing, S.J. (2014) 'Enabling young children's participation in decision-making.' SSSC News, June edn. Accessed on 26/06/2017 at http://ssscnews.uk.com/2015/05/04/enabling-young-childrens-participation-decision-making.
3. Johnson, J.A. and Dinger, D. (2012) Let Them Play: An Early Learning (Un) Curriculum. St. Paul, MN: Redleaf Press, p.1.

4. Garnett (2016).
5. Harland, J. (2017) 'A comparative study on the impact of curriculum emphasis on children's developmental patterns in an Indian and UK preschool context.' Unpublished MA research/coursework at Anglia Ruskin University.
6. Shore, R. (1997) *Rethinking the Brain: New Insights into Early Development.* New York: Families and Work Institute.
7. McMonagle, A. (2012) *Professional Pedagogy for Early Childhood Education.* County Donegal: Donegal County Childcare Committee Ltd.
8. Learning and Teaching Scotland (2005) *Let's Talk about Pedagogy: Towards a Shared Understanding for Early Years Education in Scotland.* Dundee: Learning and Teaching Scotland, p.8.

CHAPTER FIVE

Exploring the Relationship between Emotional Intelligence and Empathy

Educating the mind without educating the heart is no education at all.[1]

An educated heart is a connected one. Emotional intelligence (EI) grows when a heart is connected, and withers when a heart is neglected or disconnected. Emotional intelligence is not a luxury but a necessity. An educated heart feels supported, significant, valued and included. An uneducated heart lacks these foundational needs, and as a result, cannot learn or love in the same profound way.

In our schools, pastoral care is extremely important, but it plays second fiddle to academic outcomes. School timetables, pupil outcomes and Ofsted reports reflect this. Emotional intelligence is seen as significant, but not at the heart of education.

Sir Ken Robinson has this to say about the issue:

'We pay a high price for the exile of feeling in education. Emotional, social intelligence and inner well-being as well as academic excellence, should be carefully cultivated. For the future, it's vital to rethink the dynamic relationships between heart and mind within human consciousness and their essential place in the education of all our students.'[2]

Overlooking the emotional life of our children has indeed cost us dearly. One in four adults and one in ten children in the UK are likely to have a mental health problem in any given year. Only 25 per cent of people with mental health problems are being treated, the rest are left to cope alone. Seventy million days each year are lost due to mental ill health. The economic cost of poor mental health to the UK is somewhere between £70 and £100 billion a year.[3]

> *Science is now discovering two things that artists and spiritual leaders have always understood: that our feelings and emotions are vital to the quality of our lives and that there are intimate relationships between how we think and feel.*[4]

Education in the UK is not responsible for the deterioration in mental health but neither is it providing a lasting and effective solution.[5]

Emotional intelligence leads to good mental health. This is because people with high emotional intelligence:

- can reflect on and regulate their emotions, managing their emotional life and promoting their emotional growth

- have more empathy because they 'get' people and therefore feel connected to others

- have a higher sense of well-being and higher self-esteem.[6]

This powerful 'tool' is the cornerstone to success because people with high EI make more friends, become better leaders, have more self-confidence and perform better at work. Regardless of where we live or work, EI's influence on our mental health is crucial.

Consequently, we need to be intentional about fostering EI in the lives of children. Unless children have a profound understanding of their internal world, the emotional culture of their schools and communities will not be changed.

An emotionally intelligent culture 'grows' empathy as its natural by-product. In addition, children who understand their own feelings, and who 'get' other people are far more likely to cope more effectively with academic life. A child who does not understand his own or others' feelings will struggle with school. He will be in survival mode, very possibly leading to poor self-esteem, poor behaviour and disappointing outcomes.

A survey[7] in the USA found that teachers using social and emotional language (SEL) in school saw an increase in children's interests, better understanding and higher test scores. Academic achievement went up by an average of 11 percentile points. Teaching emotional skills led to better interaction, less aggression and better attendance. There is also an economic value. Social and emotional learning is found to show 'measurable benefits that exceed its costs, often by considerable amounts...this means that, on average, for every dollar invested equally across the six SEL interventions, there is a return of eleven dollars, a substantial economic return.'[8]

An inquiry in 2006[9] identified relationships as one of the key factors that affect mental health. Let us put relationships and connection at the heart of our curriculum. Connection promotes positive mental health, leaving children free to learn. We equip them for success.

What EI looks like

Have a look at the 'hallmarks' to EI, as recognised by Daniel Goleman, psychologist and author of *Emotional Intelligence: Why It Can Matter More Than IQ*[10] (see Figure 5.1).

This is a winning combination. It describes someone we may picture as a great leader. The truth is that this could be any one of us; we are all capable of growing strong EI. It is a skill that is open to everyone, everywhere.

Emotional intelligence requires practice. When we know what our feelings are, we can 'label' them, and so the emotion becomes a recognised 'feeling'. At that point we can begin to understand the feeling, to compare it to other feelings we've experienced and to analyse it. We can take control. It is only then that we can 'regulate' the emotions. By continually practising this process we can become emotionally intelligent.

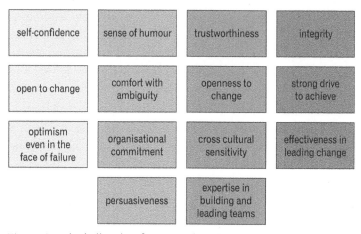

Figure 5.1 The hallmarks of emotional intelligence

We are all emotional beings, and our feelings are crucial to our healthy development. They affect how we learn and develop, with the most critical window of learning taking place in infancy and early childhood. Preschool is the optimum zone of learning for EI; at no other point in a child's life is the potential for healthy development so profound.

How emotionally intelligent is *your* setting?

Are you functioning as an emotionally intelligent setting? We can only foster EI when we possess it ourselves. This is a sobering thought. It is not possible to build EI when emotional stability and security are lacking. We hold a significant chunk of our preschoolers' emotional lives in our hands – our emotional health is key to their success.

Table 5.1 compares the benefits of strong or high EI with the inadequacies of weak or low EI.

Table 5.1 Comparing high with low emotional intelligence

	Self-awareness	Use of emotions	Understanding and analysing emotions	Managing emotions
High EI	I know how I am feeling and share these feelings when necessary with people around me	I deal with difficult feelings even though it is unpleasant at the time. I know that the feelings will fade	I can express myself in situations where there is distress or anxiety. I can see the whole picture, and this helps keep me objective	I can override negative feelings, even when caught off guard
Low EI	I am not always aware of my feelings, or am often reluctant to share them	I find it difficult to deal with my feelings and tend to resort towards self-comforting behaviours, some of which are negative, such as food or alcohol	I find it difficult to express myself, and as a result, I tend to be overwhelmed, passive or even aggressive	I am a victim to any negative feelings, especially when caught off guard

We take for granted that teachers will have strong EI but this may not always be the case, particularly when the work place becomes stressful and staff are overworked. However, there is a very clear correlation between placing EI at the centre of learning, and a peaceful setting that aids children in developing healthy connections.

Emotional intelligence requires a healthy support system. It cannot be developed in isolation. Early years settings are based on team teaching, and this provides the ideal platform for mutual support and constructive feedback.

Self-assessment and EI go hand in hand. When we reflect on our emotional responses, incidences and experiences in the setting, we will start to see how all-encompassing EI is. We can learn to become more sensitive and aware. Sensitivity and awareness stabilise the emotional atmosphere, and are the basis to an emotionally healthy classroom.

How do we go about this?

Let's take a look at the following components of EI, answering the questions:

SELF-AWARENESS

- Do I recognise what I am feeling?
- Do I recognise what the children are feeling?
- Do I notice when I/the children are bored, angry or sad?
- Do I know what triggers these feelings?
- How do I respond?
- Am I positive or negative in my response?

Look out for: tone of voice, facial expressions, body language, lack of laughter and humour in yourself and others.

USE OF EMOTIONS

- In terms of the six basic human emotions of joy, anger, sadness, disgust, fear and surprise, to what intensity do I feel these emotions on a day-to-day basis?
- How do I convey these emotions to other people?
- Do I let my feelings run riot, without stopping to think about the effect on other people?
- Do I allow my feelings to guide my thinking?
- Do I use my feelings to help me make decisions?
- Am I able to see more than one point of view?

Look out for: increased negative behaviour and a dip in creativity all round. Are you or the children 'overloaded' or dealing with too much stress?

UNDERSTANDING AND ANALYSING EMOTIONS

- Can I express myself, finding the right words to say?
- Can I help the children to express themselves, finding the right words to say?
- Do I understand why children behave in a certain way?
- Can I look objectively at the 'whole' child, seeing them in terms of their development and not in terms of their immediate behaviour?

Look out for: signs that the children do not understand what you, or others, are feeling; negative behaviour; lack of eye contact; and avoidance in talking or communicating.

MANAGING EMOTIONS

- Can I move from a negative feeling to a positive one on my own?
- When I am caught off guard, do I say things that I regret later?
- Can I override more persistent negative feelings?
- Do I process how I manage my feelings for future reference/action?

Look out for: unexpected, negative feelings that affect any activity you are involved in. Are your powerful feelings influencing other people's behaviour?

Emotional intelligence flourishes when it becomes the culture of the setting and is not simply part of a curriculum. Such an emotional-rich culture empowers children, enabling them to become emotionally 'smart'.

However, there are serious blocks to 'growing' EI, and these have a damaging effect on children and their mental health. They are *stress* and *low-level well-being*. These two elements are dangerous and persistent. Society allows them to fester, and they rob children of their peace, act as a threat to their happiness and stall their learning.

Let's take a look at the brain. This is where it all starts.

Stress and amygdala hijack

The human brain hasn't had a hardware upgrade in about 100,000 years.[11]

The plain fact is that emotions exist in our bodies, not in our heads. We don't ever 'feel' with our minds. Emotions relentlessly course through us, expressed through our quickened heart rate, sweaty palms and our need for fight or flight. We can't override these primal reactions, and sometimes they can be extremely unpleasant. We will go to extraordinary lengths to avoid such responses, often resulting in addictions and mental disorders. Until we are able to master our responses, we will be the victim of them.

Deep within our brain is the amygdala. We need this small, almond-shaped set of neurons to help us process emotions. Essentially, the amygdala responds to any potential threat. It 'remembers' unpleasant or fearful triggers and activates the release of chemicals that make us experience the 'fight or flight' sensations, such as increased heart rate, or an urge to run.

The amygdala works at lightning speed! This 'emotive' part of our brain responds a hundred times faster than our thinking brain. As a result, whenever we feel frightened or angry *we lose our capacity to think clearly because the amygdala halts all thought.*

And so, when someone makes us jump by leaping out at us in the dark, the amygdala 'remembers' the danger of footsteps and releases stress chemicals, which increase the heart rate. Our second response is to either run like crazy, or stand and fight. There is no logical thought process here. Instead we experience what is known as an *amygdala hijack.*

Our thinking brain is hijacked. We become 'unthinking' and as a result, potentially unpredictable. When Mike Tyson famously bit Evander Holyfield's ear, he was not thinking clearly. It was an expensive loss of judgement because it cost him $3 million dollars and his reputation. He was experiencing an amygdala hijack.

When the amygdala is active, it releases all sorts of stress chemicals into our blood stream, and these can remain there for up to four hours. Gradually the working memory clears. We calm down, and normal behaviour resumes. Have you ever sent an email while you are angry, and then bitterly regretted it? Or thought of a really good stinging retort about half an hour after a good argument? You've experienced a dose of amygdala hijack!

Amygdala hijack can have serious consequences. If we temporarily suspend our better judgement during a bout of anger, we stand to lose more than just our temper.

Children who experience stress and anxiety early on in life are more at risk of developing depression and other anxiety disorders when they are adults. The size of their amygdala actually grows when there is an excess of anxiety and stress.[12] They are slaves to anxiety, tied down by stress.

Preventing stress

There is such a thing as *healthy stress.* We all need a little bit of it to get us out of bed in the mornings. Healthy stress helps us to develop grit and perseverance. It is only when stress becomes excessive or disproportionate that it is a cause for concern.

Typical negative stress reactions happen when children are miserable, tired or anxious. They may begin to behave differently, becoming hyperactive and 'silly'. They may be defensive, have less motivation or find it hard to focus. Some may engage in conflict, others will be hard to please. Others may appear wary and watchful.

This is where EI is vital. It is the life support system for connection. *There are many children who are unable to stop stress in its tracks.* They don't have the relevant maturity or the right support. What happens then? They are loaded with *chronic stress*, which can affect every system in their body, from their nervous system to their gastrointestinal system. Even their muscles can be affected. Such stress creates profound and damaging trauma.

Illness, divorce and bereavement are all highly stressful occurrences and children can potentially become very withdrawn or clingy as a result. Likewise, many children find any sort of change stressful. The most common type of stress in young children is separation anxiety and we witness this on a daily basis in our early years settings.

So how do we cope with such stress? How do we reduce occasionally high levels of it in our setting? How do we support the children who are suffering from an overload of stress in their lives?

Strategies for preventing stress

Children who are upset, frightened or angry cannot play in a normal or appropriate manner. Nor can they think or connect healthily. Their amygdala is busy pumping stress hormones into their bodies and their thinking brains have been hijacked.

This is how we should respond.

Listen/connect

The power of being heard is immense. Sometimes this is all it takes to bring a highly stressed child down to normal levels of stress. The initial problem is that the child may feel stuck on one side of the emotional 'wall' with the practitioner on the other side. There is a disconnection. But once the child feels connected to the practitioner, some of the power and intensity of the feelings he is experiencing may subside.

This is not about trying to get the child to 'get over' the feeling as quickly as possible. It is about listening to the child as he processes it. This may take 20 seconds, one minute or one hour. But once we become responsive to the child's feelings, however intense, the child's stress levels can start to come down, and he will feel calmer.

Connection is also about warmth and positive touch. A hug, a fist bump or a 'high five' says more than a multitude of words. In addition, positive touch actually reduces stress hormones, and releases other hormones that make us feel better.

Label feelings

'You are sad because Mummy has left.'

Children often *don't know what they are feeling!* Imagine that! They are being consumed by a strong feeling that they don't recognise or understand. It is both scary and stressful. How do we help them?

We teach the child the language of emotion, just as we would teach them French or Spanish. When we learn more vocabulary in a language, we can start to practise speaking it in context. The more we practise, the more fluent we become. The same goes for EI. The more a child can practise 'speaking' the language, the more 'fluent' he will become. Thus, when we *label feelings* by giving them a name, we are gradually building up the child's emotional vocabulary and fluency. We are growing their EI.

Validate feelings

A little girl is playing, and another child takes her toy. She starts to cry. We can comfort the feeling, deny it or validate it.

Validating involves making a statement: 'I can see that you are very cross about your toy.' We are not trying to fix the child and make the feeling better. We are simply telling him that it is acceptable to feel what he is feeling.

Children learn to become resilient when they have worked through a feeling from the moment the feeling begins until its resolution, or their successful management of it. Sometimes they need support to do this. At other times they can do it on their own. I have witnessed children on countless occasions sorting out a conflict issue simply because their feelings have been validated, and there is an atmosphere of support and encouragement.

Offer empathy

Empathy is a process, starting with recognition of the other's pain, stepping into their shoes, and thinking about the best possible solution for them and not oneself. It takes time, energy and a large dose of EI. This is not always easy to do in a busy setting when other issues vie for a practitioner's attention. Simply by being present and available, we will help lower the stress levels that the child is experiencing. However, when we skip this process, and start trying to offer solutions before the child understands what he is feeling, we miss out the vital part of the procedure, the recognition and acceptance of feelings. Spend time on this process. It cannot be hurried.

Be present

The single best predictor of how well children turn out in the end is the secure attachment with at least one person in their early years. When we are stressed, our instinct is to go to the people we are closest to. This helps us to feel safe and secure. When a child is overwhelmed with feelings, it is enough for them to be able to seek you out and come to you. The disconnect he feels in his brain will subside, and the stress hormones will start to decrease.

Our well-being

Our well-being affects our mental health. When we have high levels of well-being, we are happy and full of energy. This is because well-being positively affects our self-confidence and self-assurance.

There is more. When we are in a good mood, we are generally able to exercise better judgement. This is important in our work with young children every day. Our very mood affects the way we relate, the way we make judgements and the way we make decisions. *The emotional state of teachers directly affects the emotional lives of children in their care.* Teachers will grade essays differently if they are in a 'positive emotion condition' as opposed to a 'negative emotion condition'.[13]

We can measure the well-being of the children in our setting by using the Leuven Scale for Well-being (see Table 5.2).

Table 5.2 The Leuven Scale for Well-being

Level	Well-being	Signals
1	Extremely low	The child clearly shows signs of discomfort such as crying or screaming. He may look dejected, sad, frightened or angry. The child does not respond to the environment, avoids contact and is withdrawn. The child may behave aggressively, hurting himself or others.
2	Low	The posture, facial expression and actions indicate that the child does not feel at ease. However, the signals are less explicit than under Level 1 or the sense of discomfort is not expressed the whole time.
3	Moderate	The child has a neutral posture. Facial expression and posture show little or no emotion. There are no signs indicating sadness or pleasure, comfort or discomfort.
4	High	The child shows obvious signs of satisfaction (as listed under Level 5). However, these signals are not constantly present with the same intensity.
5	Extremely high	The child looks happy and cheerful, smiles, cries out with pleasure. He may be lively and full of energy. Actions can be spontaneous and expressive. The child may talk to himself, play with sounds, hum, sing. The child appears relaxed and does not show any signs of stress or tension. He is open and accessible to the environment. The child expresses self-confidence and self-assurance.

The Leuven Scale is a useful tool for practitioners. A child high on the well-being scale will be more involved, leading to further deep-level learning. His attitude will be generally positive, with social interactions having a better chance of success. He will therefore generally make better judgements.

Conversely, a child low in well-being will find it difficult or even impossible to become involved, and learning will be reduced dramatically. The child will effectively be locked into the amygdala hijack mode, where the thinking brain cannot function properly and judgements will therefore be negatively affected.

Raising levels of well-being and involvement

Studies demonstrate that 'levels of well-being and involvement can be raised significantly in less than one year even in settings situated in deprived areas'.[14]

Gathered together by a 'myriad of experiences' by practitioners and teachers, the following *Ten Action Points*[15] support the development and increase of well-being in the early years classroom.

1. **Create a rich environment.** Keep the classroom attractive with appealing corners and areas. Throw out tired displays, activities or equipment. Bring in different and enticing toys, activities and learning zones.

2. **Enrich these areas.** Observe the room through the eyes of a newcomer. Be vigilant about enhancing what you already have.

3. **Introduce new/unconventional materials and activities.** Stimulate the children's interests with activities that encourage questions and experimentation.

4. **Be vigilant in observing children.** Discover the children's interests, and find activities that meet and extend those interests.

5. **Support ongoing activities through stimulating impulses and enriching interventions.** Suggest activities to the children and ask thought-provoking questions. Let the children experiment, investigate and explore.

6. **Widen the possibilities for free initiative.** Respect the children's initiatives. Support the children with sound rules and agreements. Talk through these processes.

7. **Support and encourage the emotional climate and positive relations.**

8. **Explore the world of feelings, behaviour and values.**

9. **Identify children with emotional challenges** and create sustaining and ongoing intervention.

10. **Identify children with developmental challenges** and create sustaining and ongoing intervention.

There is strong evidence that these types of experiential 'active ingredients' create involvement in the classroom. Crucially, adults need to interact with children through *stimulation, sensitivity and giving autonomy*.[16]

Adults *stimulate* by suggesting exciting and inspiring activities to children, by offering rich information, thought-provoking questions and shared thinking.

Sensitivity is demonstrated through empathy, understanding the child in full, not in part.

Giving autonomy is established when adults give and respect a child's initiative. It is demonstrated when adults acknowledge children's interests and let them experiment, choosing the way an activity will take place and the rules necessary to make the activity work best.[17]

High levels of well-being create an involved, motivated child. We know that well-being grows best in settings that encourage children to initiate and explore in experiential learning. Such learning activates and enriches a learning vitality in children and 'draw[s] them into a positive spiral which engenders deep level learning'.[18]

Conclusion

Education tends to be standardised as opposed to personalised. It repeatedly demands conformity. It is usually data driven with social and emotional learning considered to be 'soft skills' rather than an essential part of the curriculum.

We teach children to look outwards, towards exam results and future choices, all based on their performance levels. The inner world of the child is often neglected.

When do our children have the opportunity to work out what it is they love to do, or feel passionate about? When do they begin to understand what triggers them emotionally and how to manage these feelings? Their time is spent on academic subjects and there is often too much to learn, with too many exams to pass – and there is too much stress to deal with.

> *If your emotional abilities aren't in hand, if you don't have self-awareness, if you are not able to manage your distressing emotions, if you can't have empathy and have effective relationships, then no matter how smart you are, you are not going to get very far.*[19]

Fostering emotional intelligence is not just a soft, fluffy option. Emotional intelligence can and will influence children's future levels of success, and affect their choices. It will reflect in their personal history and in their relationships. When a child learns that feelings come and go, and that strategies to help manage them can be put into place, the whole world opens up to him, a safe, self-regulated, autonomous world.

No longer is a child a victim of their feelings. He is in charge. He has good mental health.

Notes

1. Aristotle, 384–322 BC, ancient Greek philosopher.
2. Robinson, K. (2011) Educating the Heart and Mind. Dalai Lama Center Speakers Series.
3. McManus, S., Meltzer, H., Brugha, T., Bebbington, P. and Jenkins, R. (2009) *Adult Psychiatric Morbidity in England: Results of a Household Survey.* The NHS Information Centre for Health and Social Care. Accessed on 26/06/2017 at http://content.digital.nhs.uk/catalogue/PUB02931/adul-psyc-morb-res-hou-sur-eng-2007-rep.pdf.
4. Robinson, K. and Aronica, L. (2014) *Finding Your Element: How to Discover your Talents and Passions and Transform your Life.* London: Penguin, p.98.
5. Sir Ken Robinson, writer and education specialist.
6. Burrus, J., Betancourt, A., Holtzman, S., Minsky, J., MacCann, C. and Roberts, R.D. (2012) 'Emotional intelligence relates to well-being: Evidence from the situational judgment of emotional management.' *Applied Psychology: Health and Well-Being 4,* 151–166.
7. Durlak, J.A., Weissberg, R.P., Dymnicki, A.B., Taylor, R.D. and Schellinger, K.B. (2011) 'The impact of enhancing students' social and emotional learning: A meta-analysis of school-based universal interventions.' *Child Development 82,* 1, 405–432.
8. Belfield, C., Bowden, B., Klapp, A., Levin, H., Shand, R. and Zander, S. (2015) 'The economic value of social and emotional learning.' *Journal of Benefit-Cost Analysis 6,* 3, p.5.
9. Lee, M. (2006) 'Promoting mental health and well-being in later life.' Age Concern and the Mental Health Foundation. Accessed on 26/06/2017 at https://www.mentalhealth.org.uk/sites/default/files/promoting_mh_wb_later_life.pdf.
10. Goleman, D. (1996) *Emotional Intelligence: Why It Can Matter More Than IQ.* London: Bloomsbury. Used by kind permission of Daniel Goleman.
11. Daniel Goleman, psychologist and science journalist.
12. Cohen, M.M., Jing, D., Tottenham, N., Lee, F.S. and Casey, B.J. (2013) 'Early-life stress has persistent effects on amygdala function and development in mice and humans.' *Proceedings of the National Academy of Sciences of the United States of America 110,* 45, 18274–18278.
13. Marc, A., Brackett, Floman, J.L., Ashton-James, C., Cherkasskiy, L. and Salovey, P. (2013) 'The influence of teacher emotion on grading practices: A preliminary look at the evaluation of student writing.' *Teachers and Teaching: Theory and Practice, 19,* 6, 634–646.
14. Laevers, F. (2015) *Making Care and Education More Effective Through Well-Being and Involvement: An introduction to Experiential Education.* Belgium: Center for Experiential Education. Accessed on 27/07/2017 at https://vorming.cego.be/images/downloads/Ond_DP_IntroductionExpEduc.pdf, p.3.
15. Laevers (2015).
16. Laevers, F., Bogaerts, M. and Moons, J. (1997) *Experiential Education at Work: A Setting with 5-year-olds.* Leuven, Belgium: Centre for Experiential Education.

17. Laevers, F. (2005) *Deep-level-learning and the Experiential Approach in Early Childhood and Primary Education.* Belgium: Research Centre for Early Childhood and Primary Education. Accessed on 27/07/2017 at https://vorming.cego.be/images/downloads/BO_DP_Deep-levelLearning.pdf.
18. Laevers (2005).
19. Daniel Goleman.

CHAPTER SIX

How Conflict and Conflict Resolution Produce Empathetic Children

The role of conflict

Conflict is inevitable. It presents itself in many forms, typically starting with clashing beliefs or views and ending with an expression of feelings, sometimes in violence. In short, conflict can be highly destructive.

And yet conflict is also necessary and desirable. When we are intentional and purposeful about dealing with conflict, we provide a windfall of positive outcomes for the children in our care.

> Conflict can increase achievement, motivation to learn, higher-level reasoning, long term retention, healthy social and cognitive development, and the fun students have in school. Conflict can enrich relationships, clarify personal identity, increase ego strength, promote resilience in the face of adversity, and clarify how one needs to change.[1]

Interestingly, conflict itself is not the problem. It is the way we process it which causes distress. Conflict resolution skills are born out of the simple desire to reduce a threat. Although conflict is inevitable, the real issue lies in how we manage it, how we move towards a peaceful solution. This is a crucial learning process.

The role of adults is central to conflict resolution. When adults help young children to acknowledge the pain of conflict and to work though this pain to reach a peaceable conclusion, children are empowered. They learn to *think* through personal distress towards a *solution*.

The transformative power of *connection* changes the dynamics of conflict into something positive and upbeat. Connection is the game changer, the hidden weapon in dealing with conflict and disagreement. Connection requires us to see the perspective of the other. I have seen storms in a teacup dissipate within seconds once a child is shown the perspective of another.

The culture of connection opens doors. Disconnection closes them. It really is that simple. Virtually all conflict resolution depends on thinking skills – the understanding of what has happened and what could happen next, and the choosing of the best possible solution. When children are supported in developing these skills (and it may take a couple of decades for them to do so) they will learn about cooperation, taking responsibility, self-control, assertion and empathy.

Conflict is never pleasant, but when children realise that it *can* be managed and dealt with, it transforms both their play and their lives. They start to grow life skills that are central to future happiness and success.

Conflict starting point

Each child has a conflict 'starting point'. Her temperament and any early experiences of conflict will influence these starting points. Positive or negative experiences of conflict will affect a child's dispositions and her core beliefs about her life. As a result, a child will have developed some sort of primary conflict strategy. This could be assertion or withdrawal, aggression or passivity. Practitioners need to understand the child's temperament, dispositions and experience of conflict in order to appreciate the child's conflict starting point.

Let's take a look at them in turn.

Temperament

A child's temperament has a powerful influence on future learning. We all have a set of these innate traits. Generally speaking, they fall into three categories:

- Easy: a child who is generally in a positive mood, who adapts quickly to new situations and forms routines easily.

- Difficult: a child who tends to react negatively, cries frequently and finds routines and new experiences challenging.

- Slow to warm up: a child who can be negative about new experiences and finds it hard to adapt, while remaining low in intensity.

Our temperament is part of our personality, and largely determines how we go about living and learning. However, the plasticity of the brain means that *adults can affect a child's temperament by what they say and how they say it.* A pattern of responses from an adult will create a pattern of responses in the child. The brain wires it that way.

A 'good fit' of temperament is therefore vital for a child's well-being and development. A 'good fit' is the compatibility between the environment and the child, where the temperament is both understood and accommodated. This is easier said than done. A child with irregular eating and sleeping patterns, coupled with negative mood swings and a tendency to withdraw will be far more challenging than a predictable child with a positive mood state.

The challenge for us is in how we respond to children. Once again it is down to connection. We may not be able to change a temperament, but we can acknowledge it and work with it. Good fits create positive brain connections. Bad fits break them. We can have a powerful influence on children by observing, respecting and working with their individual temperaments. Let's make sure we get it right.

Dispositions

Every child and practitioner has a different set of 'beliefs' about life. These are reflected in our patterns of behaviour and in our ways of thinking. They are called *dispositions*.

Dispositions are internalised 'habits of mind'. They reflect the way we have responded to life's experiences to date. If life is generally good, our dispositions will reflect that. If life is difficult, chances are that dispositions will be negative. They form the attitude of the 'half full' or 'half empty' cup. They are strengthened or weakened in proportion to the amount of positivity or negativity in the environment.

Positive dispositions include:

- Curiosity: a child has learned that following her interest, supported by an adult, can lead to fun and enjoyment.

- Persistence: the child has experienced finishing a challenging task with the help (scaffolding) of an adult, and knows that this produces a good feeling.

- Involvement: the child has enjoyed moments of intense concentration, which is a reward in itself.

- Taking responsibility: the child has reached an understanding of an activity or event, and can take part in the joint responsibility of it.

Negative dispositions include:

- Dependence: a child lacks key independence skills.

- Impatience: a child has developed negative coping skills.

- Lack of motivation: a child has had limited experiences of deep involvement activities, and therefore lacks the drive to achieve.

Some dispositions are *inborn*, where babies are naturally curious or determined. Then there are the *intellectual dispositions*, also innate, where children enjoy learning new things. These can be neglected, or damaged due to a lack of opportunity. Lastly, there are the *social dispositions*, which are acquired by being with other people. Again, these grow or diminish according to the quality of these interactions. There is a strong correlation between healthy peer interactions and emotional, cognitive and even moral development.

These dispositions are the bedrock to social cohesion. A curious, persistent, involved and responsible individual has huge value in society. Not only is she able to give back what she has received, but also she is able to contribute a great deal more to her future family and community, considered by many to be the pinnacle of success.

A child's early experiences of conflict

This is challenging. We cannot know exactly the state of a child's mind, and we won't know for sure the depth of a child's experiences of conflict. And yet it is the very nature of these conflicts that will underpin the child's ability to manage future disputes and disagreements. Children exposed to unresolved and destructive conflict between parents are more at risk of emotional and behavioural difficulties. They struggle to make healthy relationships. They are less likely to settle at preschool, will have problems sleeping, and will be more likely to suffer from poorer health.[2]

When we realise that a child may be experiencing conflict at home, we can support her in more significant ways. Children don't get used to conflict. If anything, they become more and more sensitive and vulnerable. They are at risk of reduced emotional, physical and social health. Early years practitioners are in a key position to identify such conflict and to provide the essential support the child needs. The negative impact of conflict can then be reduced. This is a critical role.

Resolving conflict

Children cannot master conflict resolution without the presence of conflict.

If conflict were absent, 'children would not learn important life skills such as judging emotional interactions with others, learning personal boundaries, facing future problems, and learning important conflict resolution skills'.[3]

Conflict resolution plays a far-reaching, vital role in human development. Resolving conflict reduces stress, heals rifts and strengthens friendships. Children need to practise conflict resolution many hundreds of times. In this way they can, with support, work out strategies for dealing with many different types of conflict.

Such conflict resolution strategies and/or collective 'wisdom' is stored in the left side of the brain. The right side of the brain, on the other hand, is more impulsive and reactive. The amygdala, a small pearl sized section of the brain, releases cortisol, and shuts down thought processes. The amygdala responds in just a few thousandths of a second to a threatening situation and is entirely action based.

Conflict releases cortisol and this shuts down the ability to think clearly. Inexperienced, untrained children tend to rely on their right hemisphere to deal with conflict. Their thought processes shut down. Stress hormones flood their bodies. At this point, the presence of a supportive adult is vital as children are less able to manage conflict if there is limited adult support.

Children learn to problem solve and to cooperate when adults support and guide them through the conflict process. This promotes the *thinking environment* necessary for conflict resolution. Once stress is reduced, thinking and resolving can follow. Our knowledge of this process is essential. Research is clear that when teachers have more skills in conflict resolution training, children have more skills in generating their own solutions, and rely more on relevant 'thinking' solutions and less on forceful 'action' ones.[4]

Simple and elaborate conflict

In every conflict there are two opposing 'goals'. The goal of one of the children may be to keep a toy, or make a new friend, while the other child's aim or goal will differ. Whatever the situation, the two children's intentions will be contradictory or even incompatible.

During conflict, children instinctively respond by mimicking their 'opponent' who becomes the role model. As a result, a child's strategies in conflict are largely influenced by the other child's strategies. When the 'opponent' responds aggressively, the other child will generally react accordingly.

Such conflicts are 'simple'. They can escalate fast because there is no place for compromise or cooperation.

'I want it. It's mine.'

'It's mine, I want it.'

Likewise, such conflicts can also de-escalate fast.

In other words, as children receive 'cues' they react to those cues accordingly. These cues may either activate hostility, or facilitate goodwill and agreeableness.

Elaborate conflict, on the other hand, contains reasoning and to some extent, compromise. The child starts to see the other's perspective. There is connection. As a result, conflict resolution becomes more likely. The difference between simple and elaborate conflict is the absence or presence of rational strategies.

Generally speaking, children veer towards the simple conflict strategy of insistence, where one child wins and the other loses. However, with the support of an adult, the central role of 'thinking' about conflict can be interwoven into the conflict, thereby changing the outcome. Once a child starts *thinking* about the conflict, her stress is reduced and a resolution is possible.

Anticipating conflict

Conflict happens. Child to child, simple or elaborate, conflict will take place in every setting, every day. During one recent study of conflict in preschoolers, 322 out of 400 observations of children generated some sort of conflict incident.[5]

When we anticipate conflict and prepare well for it, we provide the first steps in conflict resolution. However, if we consider conflict to be a problem, one that interferes with our daily experiences, we miss out on the essential nature of conflict: as a central part of a child's learning.

We can prepare for conflict in the setting. Pre-emptive, responsive and intentional strategies to create and build a climate of social acceptance and friendship are key in using empathy to build a positive approach to conflict.

Responsive and approachable environments tend to generate a gentle range of conflict strategies. Loud and aggressive environments generally result in a loud and aggressive range of strategies. In short, a positive emotional environment needs to be *respectful and responsive.*

A *respectful* adult is effective in managing conflict because she creates a positive learning experience through the utilisation of a gentle, consistent approach. For example, if an adult picks up a child from behind, without any warning, the child may find that approach unnerving and unpredictable. A respectful adult will tell or show the child what is going to happen. Respect is reliable and predictable. Through respect, the child will feel safe.

Responsiveness helps to create a warm and nurturing environment that feels safe and secure. A responsive environment is one that is filled with dependable adults who provide sensitive and encouraging interactions. These interactions need to be continuous and compelling, with plenty of direct eye contact, smiling and laughing. Such responsiveness helps practitioners to be in tune with the children, recognising and understanding their cues, such as gestures, facial expressions and body language.

There is a range of factors that can change the emotional atmosphere. Children can be both independent and dependent, easy going or difficult, within the same five minutes. They can be volatile and unpredictable. Other factors that influence the emotional atmosphere of a setting include the ratio of boys to girls, how many younger children or new children are present, and if there are children who are coping with stressful home situations, such as moving home, divorce or bereavement. This range of behaviours can be challenging for the practitioner. Responsiveness reduces the ill effects of these varying factors and can increase positive outcomes.

Use of space

The physical space of a classroom has a considerable impact on child development and behaviour. When a room is laid out with interesting and enticing areas, including ones that are quiet and ones that are busy, the child can choose where to be and can also learn how to behave in those spaces. A large empty space can allow the children too much freedom of movement, causing havoc. Too little space can lead to chaos because the children feel cramped and agitated. When we anticipate what might happen in a space, we can prepare more effectively.

The organisation of a space can also have a direct impact on any conflict. Too many children at the water table will mean that they may find it harder to cooperate. Not enough space between activity areas may mean that children cannot move freely. When we intentionally and wisely plan the use of space, children can use the space more spontaneously and instinctively, which makes conflict less likely to occur.

What are the key conflict strategies and how do we apply them?

Children need to learn self-control, empathy, compassion, patience, social etiquette, and an upbeat, constructive attitude for dealing with social problems.[6]

Young children do not set out to be unkind or hurtful. They are simply goal orientated, focused on getting a favourite toy or sitting next to their best friend. Peace building requires consistency, communication and predictability. Practitioners need to be gently responsive in the heat of a conflict, always dealing with it immediately in order to prevent the conflict from escalating.

This creates an atmosphere of 'expectedness'. Children know what is happening, what is going to happen next and what tends to 'always' happen. This reduces stress and helps to create a good pro-social atmosphere.

The following conflict resolution strategies work! Children respond to the empathetic and constructive approach. Stress and anxiety are reduced as each child is heard, understood and respected in turn.

Here is the process to follow in resolving conflict in young children:

- **Eye contact:** Practitioners need to get down to the children's eye level. If they stand over the children, they may have the height advantage, but they may have lost the emotional connection with the child. Non-threatening body language combined with eye contact is powerful; it encourages the child to relax, to connect and to attend to what you are saying. This is the best possible start.

- **Find out what has happened:** At this stage, the practitioner is not trying to find an answer or to solve the problem. They are simply gathering all of the information together. Once this is done, the practitioner paraphrases what was heard. Restating the problem back to the children is key. It tells the children that the practitioner has heard the problem, and is helping them to find solutions.

Conflict resolution depends on good communication skills. Children with poor language will find it harder to communicate the 'thinking' part of this strategy. It is vital that they are given ways of communicating, so that they do not miss out (scenario/conflict cards, sign language, etc.).

At this point each child learns of the other's perspective. This brings new understanding to the conflict.

- **Think of a solution:** This is the crucial part of the process. The practitioner asks all of the children involved in the problem *to think of a solution together*. Such scaffolding builds vital thinking skills. The solutions may not be 'right' or 'good'. It doesn't matter. This is a learning process. Practitioners need to praise all thinking, and help find a solution from the shared thinking of the children.

  Children need to be exposed to hundreds of occasions where they can practise these types of thinking skills. It is highly repetitive, and can feel unrewarding, but each experience, *supported by a warm and responsive adult*, brings the children nearer to emotional and social cohesion.

- **Stand back and watch:** Praise the children as the solution unfolds. If it doesn't happen immediately, go back to the eye contact stage, and find out again what has happened. Adults need to respond swiftly and calmly each time, and to support the children until a solution has been found. It may feel repetitive and boring, *but it empowers the children in terms of being active participants in the conflict resolution process, thereby giving them further agency and 'voice'*.

Once the solution appears to be working, praise the children for their good thinking, for making the proposed solution work. Such praise builds up their sense of competence and confidence. They will take that positive disposition with them to the next conflict (see Figure 6.1).

Underpinning these strategies is the *development of language*, which is central to conflict resolution. Talking, reading and laughing together are powerful influences in language development. When we routinely discuss feelings and opinions, providing children with an emotions-based vocabulary, we create a healthy forum for conflict resolution. This type of language becomes familiar to the child, and when used in a high state of stress and conflict, can be highly effective in lowering stress levels and restoring peace.

Figure 6.1 Pyramid of conflict resolution strategies

Assertion and negotiation

A good social atmosphere is the foundation for teaching conflict management skills.[7] Furthermore, a social atmosphere works best when settings support children in being assertive.

Being assertive is not being aggressive. Neither is it about power. It is about sticking up for oneself, rather than imposing one's will on another person. Practitioners can help children to become assertive by modelling some key statements of assertion:

'Do not shout at me.'

'I am going to play here now.'

'I don't want to play with you.'

'I'm going now. I am going to tell the teacher.'

Alongside these types of assertive statement, there is assertive negotiation. We can model this for the children:

'Let's play with the toy together.'

'We can take turns.'

'I'll find you a toy like this one.'

'I see you like this toy. Would you like to play with it after I have finished?'

Practitioners are helpful when they help children talk through conflict by asserting and/or negotiating. Less effective settings have little or no follow up from negative behaviour, or distract children from negative behaviour, or simply ask children to stop. There are no lessons in this. Children might stop but it is clear that they will start up again; the cycle continues with no resolution or learning on the part of the child.

Assertion and negotiation need to become visible. Both are part and parcel of the conflict resolution process. When we assert and negotiate, acknowledging experience of conflict, understanding responses and helping with solutions, we significantly increase the children's individual and collective ability to understand how to face conflict and deal with it.

Conclusion

> *Peace has to be created, in order to be maintained. It will never be achieved through passivity and quietism.*[8]

The rate at which a child's brain is growing and forming connections during the age of two and five is phenomenal.

> Neurons are constantly affected by impulses from thousands of other neurons and, in turn, affect thousands of other neurons, etc. Through this activity millions of neurons are interconnected in vast networks that form the basis for all brain processes.[9]

The short time at preschool shapes the child's thinking and their ability to cope with conflict. The positivity or negativity of the environment can affect their brain development. Young children are at the beginning of a long journey, acquiring the complex and vital life skills of expressing feelings, resolving social difficulties and conflicts, and getting along with other people.

Empathy transforms how we handle conflict. When a child appreciates that she is different from another child, with different thoughts, feelings and views, her capacity for resolving conflict can grow.

The key conflict strategies support the development of empathy. These approaches allow the children to participate together as they gather the relevant information. It helps them see all the different perspectives of the same incident. And as they find a solution together, they are exposed once again to the perspectives of the other children, as the practitioner involves them all in the solution-finding process.

Peace is not the absence of conflict but the presence of creative alternatives for responding to conflict – alternatives to passive or aggressive responses, alternatives to violence.[10]

Our simple aim is to provide each child with relevant and personal strategies to manage conflict in their lives. The stormy sea of conflict that threatens to engulf and overwhelm can become manageable and workable.

What a gift to the children this is.

Notes

1. Broadbear, B.C. and Broadbear, J.T. (2000) 'Development of conflict resolution skills in infancy and early childhood.' *The International Electronic Journal of Health Education 3*, 4, 284–290, p.284.
2. Reynolds, J., Houlston, C., Coleman, L. and Harold, G. (2014) *Parental Conflict: Outcomes and Interventions for Children and Families.* Bristol: Policy Press.
3. Dennis, B.A., Colwell, M.J. and Lindsey, E. (2016) *Preschool Children's Conflict and Social Competence: A Comparative View.* Lubbock, TX: Texas Tech University.
4. Vestal, A. and Aaron Jones, N. (2004) 'Peace building and conflict resolution in preschool.' *Journal of Research in Childhood Education 19*, 2, p.131.
5. Chen, D.W., Fein, G.G., Killen, M. and Tam, H.K. (2001) 'Peer conflicts of preschool children: Issues, resolution, incidence, and age-related patterns.' *Early Education and Development 12*, 4, 523–544.
6. Dewar, G. (2013) 'The Dark Side of Preschool: Peers, Social Skills and Stress.' *Parenting Science.* Accessed on 26/06/2017 at www.parentingscience. com/preschool-stress.html.
7. Thornberg, R. (2006) 'The situated nature of preschool children's conflict strategies.' *Educational Psychology 26*, 1, 109–126.
8. Dorothy Thompson, 1893–1961, American journalist and broadcaster.
9. Hart, S. (2008) *Brain, Attachment, Personality: An Introduction to Neuroaffective Development.* London: Karnac Books Ltd, p.45.
10. Dorothy Thompson, 1893–1961, American journalist and broadcaster.

CHAPTER SEVEN

The Power of Positive Communication

Learning words associated with empathy and emotions helps kids learn to talk about it, it gives them legitimacy to own their emotions so they can share them. It's about connection and communication.[1]

Words encourage, comfort and inspire. Words provide relief and support. Words demonstrate and educate. Words heal. Empathetic language, planted deep into our interactions with young children, dramatically kick-starts children's ability to respond to and interact with people.

The child begins to perceive the world not only through his eyes but also through his speech.[2]

Language is acquired through the thousands of interactions we experience during our early years. These interactions influence the wiring of our brain. When the brain has positive interactions (and hears more words) brain development is healthy, allowing language skills to develop.

Early language skills and brain development literally go hand in hand. Children with good language skills are more likely to have a positive approach to learning. They listen. They enjoy the give and take of dialogue. They think. They can consider the different ideas and opinions presented by others.

Of all the literacies of childhood, emotional literacy is the most fundamental. Feelings define our similarity as humans. Our emotions are universal. The ability to find the humanity in one another will change the way that we relate to one another. It can have a huge impact on the family, by interrupting patterns of child abuse and neglect that are so often repeated through parenting in the next generation. It can have an impact on policies that lead us into conflict or compromise. It can have an impact on our very identity as citizens of the world.[3]

Connecting and tuning in to another person (cognitive empathy) requires a *language of emotions*. Cognitive empathy is a skill, and children 'acquire' it. Words matter. When children hear us using empathetic words, such as kind, safe, gentle, thoughtful, helpful, caring, listening, thinking and so on they will add them to their own inventory of words. And they will use them.

Children can effectively communicate their feelings when they have the right words: 'I feel sad because my mummy has gone.' It is not always positive: 'He took my ball. I am cross.' Through such language they can learn to recognise and understand how someone else is feeling: 'James is sad because his bike has broken.'

How do we best foster a language of emotions in our setting? First, we create an *interactive climate*, where interactions are positive and loving. Second, we regulate our *emotional climate*. Third, we plant the language of emotions in both.

Such emotional language is both verbal (including sign language) and non-verbal; and it includes facial expressions, posture, touch and laughter.

We'll take a look at each of these in turn.

The interactive climate

Have you ever been to a preschool where the air is dull and lifeless? The adults may be present but they are not fully interactive. They sit quietly on the outskirts of the children's play, offering the occasional word or comment. They yawn and look at their watches. The children 'get on' with their activities, moving from one to another, never fully immersing themselves, because the adults are not creating an interactive atmosphere. Instead they are partial observers, participating only when children become fidgety or challenging.

We know that children's outcomes are strongly influenced by the quality and range of interactions in their early years. Positive interactions create significant relationships.

No significant learning occurs without a significant relationship.[4]

Children might *survive* without such positive interactions but they won't flourish. Children only flourish in settings where adults are interested, interactive, warm and loving.

Interactive climates are highly attractive to function in because there are such strong connections between the adults and the children, and among the children themselves. In an interactive climate you will hear laughter and chatter. Children will be busy and involved. Questions, reflections and musings fill the air. Adults are placed near the children, watching carefully to work out what to do next, or they may be fully immersed in an activity. The time passes quickly. The air hums with purpose. At times a conflict may rear its head but this is often swiftly resolved, with adults quietly working on the issue with the children.

An interactive setting isn't just a tick on a list of 'outstanding' qualities in a preschool. Interaction is the lifeblood of relationships, and the cornerstone of all learning. Interaction should be a practitioner's main focus: the first step in engaging the child, not an afterthought. Once established, the interactive culture will provide an entrance for children into learning, both academic and emotional, fostering a sense of identity and purpose, and building resilience.

Emotional climate

The emotional climate is far more communicative than any words. How many times have you stepped into a room only to realise that there is a 'mood'? You can't put your finger on it, but it feels negative and unpleasant. At other times, you open a door and there is a light-hearted happiness that is almost tangible. What sets the emotional climate in a room or setting?

As people, we create a 'psychological atmosphere' around us. We take our moods into our daily lives and in this instance, into the preschool. What does your mood look like today? Have you created a positive mood despite a difficult start to the day? Have you had to fend off other people's black moods? Have you brought a negative mood into the setting, which will in turn affect others?

The emotional climate we set is crucial in that it affects everyone who comes into contact with the setting. How do we therefore create an individual and collective 'good mood' without being affected by our own and other people's negativity?

The practitioner needs to:

- be aware of any personal anxiety, tension or anger that may affect the group

- encourage both children and adults to express their moods.

Emotion cards with a mixture of faces that show pleasant and unpleasant emotions can be used for this. Everyone can take a turn in picking out a face that matches his or her particular mood. Be aware that these emotions can be high or low in energy, and this will affect the strength of the feeling. Display the faces.

In this way, everyone knows what everyone else is feeling. This daily practice helps children to understand their emotions, to 'own' what they are feeling and to express these feelings. Acknowledging these feelings and then legitimising and expressing them aids children in beginning to regulate them. This is a significant step in emotional literacy.

Verbal language of emotions (empathetic language)

Feelings are universal. First of all, children learn about their own feelings. Then they learn about the feelings of others. This teaches them about perspectives. This in turn leads towards resolving conflict. The child sees another's point of view. Emotional competence is born.

A child is generally learning words at a rapid pace while at preschool. On average this age group will be learning one new word for every two waking hours, eight words every day.[5] This is therefore the perfect opportunity to learn the language of emotions (empathy).

Affective language of emotions

Feelings are rife in the preschool setting. Children are exposed not only to their own feelings, but also to the feelings of others. Sometimes these feelings are new and overwhelming, and can be extremely unpleasant or frightening.

Labelling feelings at this age is vital. By giving a feeling a name, the child takes some control back over the feeling. For example, a child's mother leaves the room and the child cries. First the practitioner needs to label the feeling: 'You look very sad. Your mummy has left.' This is naming the scary feeling. It allows the child to claim back some control over that feeling. It may be that the child is anxious or frightened. He may not know exactly what the feeling is but what he does know is that it feels very unpleasant. Again, name the feeling for the child and explain it to him in the process: 'Your face looks worried, like this. (Copy the face.) I think that being worried may not feel very good. To help you to not feel so worried, I'm going to look after you until Mummy gets back.' The child can then identify what he is feeling. He can 'feel' what the feeling feels like – whether it is positive or negative, high or low in energy. He can be comforted by the words and actions of the adult who seeks to help him to understand and manage the feeling. He can choose to stay close to the adult until he feels ready to play.

There are a host of feelings that children may not be familiar with. These are:

- loneliness

- frustration

- rejection

- anxiety

- discouragement

- shock

- stress

- joy

- pride

- hope

- contentment

- excitement.

Name these feelings for the children. Label them as they occur in everyday situations. Approach the feelings rather like a detective: 'You have this face today. What does that mean? Are you feeling anxious, like this? (Show anxious face.)'

When we regularly examine feelings together, children become more and more emotionally literate. They understand the way that they feel, and this in turn paves the way for understanding other people's feelings.

Cognitive verbal empathy language

Once we name feelings, and begin to know what they feel and look like, we can take it a step further. We can begin to interpret them. Younger preschool children will not have reached sufficient maturity to do this yet, but we can lay the foundations for it.

Here are some useful strategies.

Stories

All stories are about different feelings and perspectives. Telling stories and reflecting on them teaches empathetic language in an enjoyable context. Read stories in groups or one to one. Leave books in role-play areas, put them in a basket out in the garden, display them in a quiet area. Reflect on the feelings and behaviours in books: 'She looks sad; her friend wasn't kind to her.' 'He is glad that his friend has come to his party.' 'She doesn't like the loud noise, it frightens her. Look at her face.' Talk about these feelings and behaviours. Ask questions such as 'What do you feel when...?' or 'What do you do when...?'

Music, songs and rhymes

Music can set the tone in a classroom. Simply having it playing quietly in the background can make a difference to the atmosphere of the room. 'Sad' music and 'happy' music can generate discussion: 'What does this music make you feel?' 'What do you want to do when you hear this song...?'

Songs and rhymes encourage children's language, but also provide opportunities to look at an array of feelings, and interpret them.

For example, sing 'How are you feeling today?' (to the tune of Hickory Dickory Dock). Use some emotion stick puppets for the children to hold while they sing. The words are as follows:

'How are you feeling today? (Repeat once)

I'm happy and glad, happy and glad,

That's how I'm feeling today.'

Repeat with 'sleepy and tired', 'grumpy and cross' or make up words that signify different feelings, for example 'whizzy and WHOO!' for excited.

Role-play
Role-play is central to children's understanding of perspectives. It deepens their own perspective and opens up other viewpoints to them.

Role-play depends heavily on language for increased play satisfaction. Practitioners need to find out what the children enjoy, and provide role-play props or materials according to those interests. Scaffold learning for the children as they enter the 'zone', for example, 'Oh! Let's make an omelette. Can you hold the spoon for me?' Use both verbal and non-verbal empathetic language: 'Oh no! Teddy is so, so sad that he can't have omelette for dinner.' 'Oh, now where is my spoon? I don't have a spoon. And I really need one to make dinner (big sigh).'

Modelling empathetic behaviour
When we demonstrate empathy, and verbalise it, we help children to become aware that feelings and behaviour are linked: 'Sally is sad, she has lost her dolly.' They start to see the reasons why people behave in a certain way: 'Sally is crying, that's because she wants her dolly back.'

It is our constant modelling and verbalising of empathy that creates an empathetic microclimate. I have known children eager to resolve conflict independently because they are familiar with the 'empathy language' that adults use and are consequently eager to give it a go.

Sign language

Signs are to eyes what words are to ears.[6]

The benefits of sign language are extensive and profound. Signing enhances language and literacy skills of preschool children particularly up to the age of six years old. Teaching children sign language creates improved communication skills, higher verbal IQ and better language skills.[7]

When children sign, they are more engaged. Studies have shown behaviour significantly improves, they concentrate for longer and they learn effortlessly, because they understand more.[8]

Empathetic sign language is powerful because it is visible. Use it in shared reading. Use it as you sing and say nursery rhymes together. Use it as you play.

This doesn't have to be a complicated and time-consuming task. Basic signs are all that are needed to get the ball rolling. Find out the signs for the familiar 'doing' words, like *play, run, walk* and *see*. Find out 'feelings' words such as *angry, sad, excited* and *happy*. Find out the signs for greeting each other and any simple known words that might be useful, such as *milk, water, lunch*, and so on. Children who are still in the initial stages of speaking rely more on non-verbal communication. Be aware of those children and use this powerful tool.

Sign language is a dance with words, to be enjoyed from babyhood through childhood to adulthood.[9]

Signing your understanding of a child's sad feeling will be soothing and calming. Signing the next transition in the day's routine will make it less stressful.

Reverend Jesse Jackson observed that, 'the hearing world does not listen'. Signing forces us to listen because it slows down the communication process, creating room for connection and empathy.

Non-verbal language of emotions

When talking about our feelings or attitudes, 90 per cent of our language is non-verbal; as a general rule, 55 per cent of it is through our facial expression, 38 per cent through the tone of our voice, and a mere 7 per cent through words.[10]

We communicate with our body posture, eye contact and tone of voice. We speak through gesture, touch and laughter. Positive non-verbal communication boosts emotional connection and sends out a message of love and acceptance. A frown or an angry tone of voice disconnects and disengages.

It seems that we get most of our social cues from non-verbal sources. Often the non-verbal and the verbal are in conflict. For example, someone says they are fine when their non-verbal language clearly states the opposite. What do we believe? *We believe the non-verbal every time.*

The power of non-verbal language is a force for good in early years settings. And yet all too often practitioners display indifference or boredom through their body language. One might ignore the excited ramblings of a three-year-old, too busy to pay attention. Another might yawn as a child proudly shows them a painting.

How much of this non-verbal language do young children understand? While they may miss the more subtle facial expressions, they will understand fully the more overt and familiar non-verbal communication, such as waving, smiling or winking.

Whenever we interact we have the opportunity to connect or disconnect through non-verbal communication. Disconnection leaves children feeling unfulfilled, without really knowing why.

Let's take a look at each of the non-verbal areas.

Facial expression

The face is a puzzle that the child tries to solve based on whatever information is available.[11]

Facial expressions are often called the key to human emotions. This is because the brain's ability to detect facial expressions is significantly quicker than processing words. *We sense the feeling faster than hearing the words.*

There are 90 or so muscles in the face and these muscles are continuously sending out a series of expressions, regardless of whether someone is there to see them or not. Our expressions display recognition, concern, pleasure, sadness and disgust. Some expressions linger, others are gone in a flash. Some are voluntary and others are involuntary.

Different parts of the brain are responsible for dealing with both the voluntary (controlled) and the involuntary (instinctive) expressions. Sometimes when we are in a highly emotional state, there is literally a tug of war on the face. The brain is simultaneously using both parts and creates a facial tussle!

From the age of two, children begin to interpret facial expressions. This consists of a 'feels good, feels bad reading' and is the building block to understanding emotions. This is why it is so important to 'label' an emotion so that it can be further identified by the child.

Practitioners need to help children to read facial expressions. This is a skill and requires practice.

'Look at Sarah's face. She looks sad.'

'What is Billy feeling? Look at his face.'

'James has a cross face.'

'Poppy's face is very happy!'

As we point out these expressions, the child learns what a feeling 'looks like'. This is emotional learning in practice.

Just as important is our reading of a child's own facial expressions. Young children express their feelings non-verbally. Watch their faces. They are open books! Children often exaggerate a facial expression to get the point across. They will 'pout' or 'grimace'. This is learned behaviour; they have worked out that an overstated facial expression gets a bigger response. These are voluntary or deliberate facial expressions. *The child wants us to see them. It is how they communicate their feelings to us.*

However, this is not always the case. What about the emotions that we miss? There are times when a child is perhaps too confused to be able to 'name' a feeling and struggles to find the right words. And there are times when a child has experienced trauma and the resulting feelings are simply too overwhelming to process. This results in the child shutting down.

Key in all of these instances is connection with the child. The well-being of a child increases when his feelings are understood, and declines when they are not. How do we foster this connection? Encourage face-to-face chat. Look into the child's eyes. Let him look into yours. In the end, it is all down to interaction. If we are not aware, we will miss important signals. If we don't look carefully, we won't see. If we don't connect, we won't understand.

And what about our own facial expressions?

The face is like a switch on a railroad track. It affects the trajectory of the social interaction the way the switch affects the path of the train.[12]

Our face is an empathy tool. Our facial expressions *influence and affect the flow of interaction.* They direct the emotional traffic.

Children respond instinctively to faces that interact and collaborate with them. Let's use our own face in this effective way, and see what happens as a result.

Body posture

Our body posture has power. Wherever we stand or sit in the setting has an effect on the other people in it. Our body posture shows how committed we are to an activity or interaction.

Body posture is usually intentional, but occasionally we are not aware of the subtle signs we are displaying. We may be speaking brightly to a child yet our body posture exhibits boredom or irritation. Such mismatching information has a negative effect on the child. He feels confused, without knowing why.

When we give all our attention to a child or children, they feel supported by us. *Body posture has the power to nurture.*

Look out for your own body language.

- Do your words match your posture?

- Does your body posture convey positivity?

- Do you face the child/ren completely, or are you partially turned away?

- Do you flinch when a child runs towards you?

- When you are playing with a child, are your arms and shoulders relaxed?

- Do you look as if you might get up and move somewhere else?

Children's thinking and behaviour are shaped by what they are feeling. When our body posture is loving and engaged it is highly likely that the child will feel content and peaceful. Their thinking and behaviour will be instinctively improved. We literally fling open wide the windows of the child's learning.

Touch

Touch is the very first of the senses to develop in the foetus, and is crucial for the baby's development. Without positive touch, babies will not thrive. We only have to think back to the stories from Romanian and Albanian orphanages where children lived with virtually no affectionate touch. The result was catastrophic for their development.

Affectionate touch is crucial for healthy development. Children who do not receive affectionate touch are more likely to be depressed, violent or ill. Lack of touch can even result in memory deficit. Children who do not receive enough affectionate touch have a brain that is more wired for aggression.

There are neurons in the brain that literally fight for supremacy: neurons for physical affection and neurons for aggression. *Affectionate contact and touch displace the neurons wired for aggression.* Touch annihilates these antisocial neurons. Likewise, not enough affectionate contact displaces the neurons specified for physical affection. This clearly has profound implications either way: 'The bottom line is that love, attention, and affection – especially physical affection – is crucial to a child's healthy development. This interaction will affect every aspect of their cognitive and emotional development going forward.'[13]

Empathy and affectionate touch are intertwined. Both are intentional and powerful. Both are responsive. Children need love, hugs and reassurance; touch encourages and enhances the secure attachment with their key person.

Cortisol, the stress hormone, rears its ugly head when a child is separated from their primary caregiver. When a child has a responsive key person, studies show that cortisol is reduced to normal levels.[14] *Touch is an essential part of this responsiveness.* Our empathy levels can be high and we can say all the right things, but without touch, the child will struggle to maintain their emotional equilibrium. The benefits of affectionate touch cannot be emphasised enough. Touch enhances healthy child development,[15] reduces anxiety and stress, increases immunity and boosts our well-being.

Affectionate touch is a valuable communication tool. It literally alters the way a brain develops. It makes empathy visible and tangible. Let's use it.

Laughter

Laughter is the shortest distance between two people.[16]

Laughter changes our mood. It releases serotonin, often called the 'happy hormone'. It builds strong connections. It induces the release of endorphins that help with pain, stress, anxiety and depression. It can even boost our immune system. What's more, laughter gives us energy and will almost always provide positive responses from adults and children alike. Laughter connects us.

Laughter has been around for about seven million years, even before man developed speech, and yet it is a phenomenon that is neglected by educators. It isn't included in national curriculums or on teaching courses. It is as if laughter is to be avoided or restricted to a 'sensible' limit or we'll all be having too much fun to be learning.

This makes no sense at all. The benefits of laughter are profound.

There is nothing in the world so irresistibly contagious as laughter and good humour.[17]

About ten years ago Thea came to our preschool. She was three years old, and did not speak at all in preschool. Her language at home was good, but she obviously found being away from home stressful and her means of coping was electing to not speak.

We tried all sorts of strategies to get Thea to talk. We discovered her interests, and followed those. We spoke with her parents. She continued to be totally silent. After a few weeks I decided to try laughter as a way to connect. I sat with Thea as she coloured in with some felt tip pens. After a minute or two I drew all over my hand with the felt tip. 'Oh, dear, what a naughty pen,' I commented to myself. The little girl looked up and I saw a smile tug at her mouth. We carried on colouring in. A minute later I drew up my arm. 'Naughty pen!' I said again, and looked at the little girl. She burst out laughing. The 'naughty pen' drew on my other hand, up my other arm, and finally drew a circle on my nose. Thea burst out laughing. 'Naughty pen!' she repeated, through her giggles. We carried on with this silliness until we were both laughing so hard that other members of staff came over to find out what was happening! From that time on, Thea spoke at preschool.

Laughter isn't just a reaction to something funny. It is a form of communication, a type of social behaviour. The laughter that Thea and I shared opened a door. Laughter is meaningless if it isn't shared. We can still laugh in isolation, but the whole point of laughter is to communicate the humour in a situation to someone else.

The frequency of *our* laughter has an effect on a *child's* laughter. A sense of humour is learned from the people around us. Children learn about their world, and understand when the world is distorted or 'wrong'. A parent might put a child's hat on. The incongruity in this will cause the child to laugh. A cartoon on television will make a preschooler laugh because of the silliness of the situation, for example, a dog mewing or a horse eating at the table. Humour works because the child understands his world, he understands what is 'normal' and therefore what is incongruous (out of place).

As practitioners, we need to be 'laughter models' in the setting. We need to take children's laughter seriously, and join in. If this becomes part and parcel of interactions in the setting, we are creating an environment that is laughter-rich. What a joyful place to work in. What a joyful place to learn in!

The effect of positive words

The mere sight of the word 'NO!' causes the release of dozens of stress hormones. This can impair all sorts of functions: our thoughts, our logic, even the way we communicate.[18] The sight of negative words to an already anxious person will make them feel a lot worse. Long-term exposure to these negative words can damage key brain structures such as memory and feelings.[19]

Each time we express negativity, stress chemicals are released, even in the listener's brain. Negativity spreads negativity.

Our inner voice can also produce more damaging neurochemicals. The internal voice tends to be much more negative than positive. This is especially true of children. It seems that negativity is part of their innate disposition. Such negativity can grow further as the child discovers the world to be a negative place.

The good news is that our genetic make-up can be altered by positivity and relaxation.[20] Epigenetics is the study of any changes in the DNA that turn genes on or off, and how cells 'read' genes. It has been discovered that positive words actually *turn on genes* that lower stress levels. We can help children develop the best possible effects of their gene pool by using positive language around them.

> By holding a positive and optimistic [word] in your mind, you stimulate frontal lobe activity. This area includes specific language centers that connect directly to the motor cortex responsible for moving you into action. And as our research has shown, the longer you concentrate on positive words, the more you begin to affect other areas of the brain... Functions in the parietal lobe start to change, which changes your perception of yourself and the people you interact with. A positive view of yourself will bias you toward seeing the good in others, whereas a negative self-image will include you toward suspicion and doubt. Over time the structure of your thalamus will also change in response to your conscious words, thoughts, and feelings, and we believe that the thalamic changes affect the way in which you perceive reality.[21]

The implications of this in preschool are profound. The more positive words we speak, the more we change the architecture of children's brains (as well as our own!). Our interactions must hum with positivity.

Key to positivity is the *environment we create*.

Seventy per cent of what is given to us genetically is brought to fruition by our environmental experiences.[22]

Whatever a child's temperament, outlook and personality, a rich and interactive environment will significantly shape their future. Happy conversations with adults and peers *wire* the brain, creating connections. Constant repetition of these pleasing experiences *reinforces* and *boosts* these connections.

What can you do?

While supportive relationships start at home, early years settings have a vital role in embedding positive communication into all daily routines and interactions. This can be done in the following ways:

- Greet each child with genuine affection each morning.

- Use the child's name: 'Remember that a person's name is to that person the sweetest and most important sound in any language.'[23]

- Use kind words; these are powerful and build up self-esteem and well-being.

- Smile! Smiling is a powerful gesture, especially when combined with positive words.

- Use positive statements to reinforce a child's behaviour: 'Nice wiping! Look how clean the table looks now.'

- Display enjoyment and pleasure in shared activities and routines.

- Model friendship with other adults, making friendship visible.

- Ask other adults for positive statements to support yours, for example, 'Look, Mrs D, have you seen Jane's painting? I love how she used the purple.' Mrs D can then reinforce what you have said in her own positive language.

- Tune into children who need extra attention. Bombard them with positive interaction and language. This helps challenging behaviour before it escalates.

- Speak positively and encouragingly throughout the day.

- Remember how effective positive language is and how it affects the brain chemistry of the children.

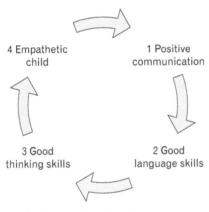

Figure 7.1 The cycle of empathetic learning

When we are intentional about positive communication, we can create a powerful thinking and speaking culture. Such a culture plants the roots of empathy and consequently grows social change. Practitioners who support a communication-rich environment create empathy through the positive words they speak and in the gentle non-verbal language they display (see Figure 7.1).

No child can have a better start than this.

Notes

1. Beach, M. (2016) 'Empathy: The Language of Emotion.' in *Teach: Education for Today and Tomorrow.* Accessed on 01/08/2017 at www.teachmag.com/archives/8946.

2. Cole, M., John-Steiner, V., Schribner, S. and Souberman, E (1978) *Mind in Society: The Development of Higher Psychological Processes.* Cambridge, MA: Harvard University Press. Accessed on 15/08/2017 at http://ouleft.org/wp-content/uploads/Vygotsky-Mind-in-Society.pdf.

3. Gordon, M. (2005) *Roots of Empathy: Changing the World Child by Child.* Toronto: Thomas Allen Publishers, p.8. Used by kind permission of Mary Gordon.

4. Comer J. (2004) *Leave No Child Behind: Preparing Today's Youth for Tomorrow's World.* London: Yale University Press, p.70.

5. Korte, M. (2001) *Wie Kinder heute lernen: Was die Wissenschaft über das kindliche Gehirn weiß.* [*How Children Learn Today: What Science Knows About the Child's Brain.*] Munich: Goldmann.

6. Glickman, K. (1999) *Deaf Proverbs.* DEAFinitely Yours Studio Wordsmith.

7. Capirci, O., Cattani, A., Rossini, P. and Volterra, V. (1998) 'Teaching sign language to hearing children as a possible factor in cognitive enhancement.' *The Journal of Deaf Studies and Deaf Education 3*, 2, 135–142.

8. Gaunt, C. (2013) 'Gove urged to introduce sign language in settings.' *Nursery* World, 23 August. Accessed on 15/08/2017 at www.nurseryworld.co.uk/nursery-world/news/1119377/gove-urged-introduce-sign-language-settings.

9. Daniels, M. (2001) *Dancing with Words: Signing for Hearing Children's Literacy.* Westport, CT: Beergin & Garvey, p.175.

10. Mehrabian, A. and Ferris, S.R. (1967) 'Inference of attitudes from nonverbal communication in two channels.' *Journal of Consulting Psychology 31*, 3, 248–252.

11. Widen, S.C. (2013) 'Children's interpretation of facial expressions: The long path from valence-based to specific discrete categories.' *Emotion Review 5*, 1, 72–77, p.73. Used by kind permission of SAGE.

12. Alan Fridlund, Associate Professor in social and clinical psychology, University of California, Santa Barbara. Used by kind permission of Alan Fridlund.

13. Global Children's Fund (n.d.) 'Child Maltreatment: A Cross-Comparison. The Importance of Touch and Physical Affection.' Accessed on 15/08/2017 at http://www.keepyourchildsafe.org/maltreatment-book/touch-affection.html.

14. Global Children's Fund (n.d.).

15. Dettling, A.C., Parker, S.W., Lane, S., Sebanc, A. and Gunnar, M.R. (2000) 'Quality of care and temperament determine changes in cortisol concentrations over the day for young children in childcare.' *Psychoneuroendocrinology 25*, 819–836.

16. Victor Borge, 1909–2000, Danish-American comedian, conductor and pianist.

17. Charles Dickens, 1812–1870, British author.
18. Newberg, A. and Waldman, M.R. (2012) *Words Can Change Your Brain: 12 Conversation Strategies to Build Trust, Resolve Conflict, and Increase Intimacy.* New York: Penguin.
19. Talarovicova, A., Krskova, L. and Kiss, A. (2007) 'Some assessments of the amygdala role in suprahypothalamic neuroendocrine regulation: a mini-review.' *Endocrine Regulations 41*, 4, 155–162.
20. Dusek, J.A., Out, H.H., Wohlhueter, A.L., Bhasin, M. *et al.* (2008) 'Genomic counter-stress changes induced by the relaxation response.' *PLoS ONE 3*, 7: e2576.
21. Newberg and Waldman (2012), pp.34–35.
22. Daniel Goleman, psychologist and science journalist.
23. Dale Carnegie, 1888–1955, American writer and lecturer.

CHAPTER EIGHT

The Significance of Pretend Play in Developing Empathy

The effects of pretend play

The more children engage in imaginative play, the more skilled they are at recognizing what others are thinking and feeling.[1]

Acts of civility are established when children pretend. Empathy, self-regulation and conflict resolution skills are built when children immerse themselves in an imaginary world. Research conclusively demonstrates that pretend play builds both affective (emotional) and cognitive thinking, and is the foundation for our ability to organise, symbolise and prioritise.

Furthermore, children love pretend play. They make cakes out of play dough, and telephones out of bananas. They drive their cars along make-believe roads and dress up as princesses and superheroes. They become mummies and daddies and go for imaginary walks in the imaginary park. They just can't help themselves. They are wired to pretend. Such play is universal, innate, untaught and spontaneous.

Pretend play is never indulgent, gratuitous or simply killing time. It is a driving need, essential for developing brain chemistry. It is generated by the child's environment, and is the primary approach that children undertake in order to make sense of the connections in their world. Children observe, notice and experiment. They mimic what they see. Consequently, children learn valuable, vital skills.

> Children's ability to engage in dramatic and sociodramatic play [is] found to be directly linked to a wealth of skills all of which are essential for academic success…good play is taught by children to one another and it is probably the necessary precursor for every other kind of learning in a classroom.[2]

Pretend play develops thinking, communication, social and negotiating skills. Children 'read' each other; they work together for the good of their shared play: 'You have this pot, and I'll have this one.' 'Can I have your cup?' 'Yes, when I have made the tea.' They pretend to be other people. This provides them with vital new perspectives. They take turns because it makes the play more satisfactory in the long run.

Furthermore, pretend play is a safe place for a child because it *feels safe*. A child can 'pretend' all sorts of calamities because the game is hers and she has control over it. The child may witness anger at home, or experience the loss of a family member. The family may be moving house, or having their home turned upside down by decorators. Pretend play helps children to work out the complicated feelings that accompany such emotional upheaval.

In order for pretend play be meaningful and successful, we need to understand the fundamental role that *attention skills*, *intrinsic motivation* and *reliable adults* have on children's learning. These three components shape a child's progress and development and have a direct influence on a child's ability to play imaginatively. Let's take a look at each in turn.

Attention skills

Attention skills are involuntary and voluntary. Involuntary (or spontaneous) attention is effortless, based on external stimuli. This is where our eye is naturally drawn to something. It appears from birth, where a baby responds to a bright light or a familiar voice.

Voluntary attention requires an effort. Despite other physical stimuli that compete for our attention we are able to stay on task. Voluntary attention emerges during the first year of life and gradually strengthens over the early years.

Joint attention, a vital stepping stone in attention skills, requires both components of attention: 'Joint attention is vital to social competence at all ages. Adolescents and adults who cannot follow, initiate, or join with the rapid-fire changes of shared attention in social interactions may be impaired in their capacity for relatedness and relationships.'[3]

This is when a child can share her focus on an object with someone else. Crucially, the child understands that the other person is also looking at the object at the same time; it is an active and intentional coordination.[4] Joint attention emerges by the end of the first year, when an infant will point to a page in a book or follow the gaze of another person.

Attention skills increase and deepen when children are motivated. Furthermore, these skills are significantly strengthened by the presence of reliable and dedicated adults. When early attention skills are encouraged and supported, they significantly influence future development. This is because attention produces *higher-level brain action*. Attention is therefore one of the key building blocks in empathy and vital for almost all interactions and relationships.

Interested children *invest* in their pretend play. They are focused and engrossed. Deep absorption in play brings immense satisfaction and joy. Quite the reverse happens with disinterested children who are likely to be stressed, anxious or overtired. Disinterested children are detached from the group and often isolated. They find it more difficult to invest in play, and will therefore have fewer opportunities to develop vital attention skills.

The best moments in our lives are not the passive, receptive relaxing times...the best moments usually occur if a person's body or mind is stretched to its limits in a voluntary effort to accomplish something difficult and worthwhile.[5]

Such high levels of engagement are favourable for both brain chemistry and future development. Studies support the view 'that paying attention and persisting on tasks are foundational skills that are critical early in life and continue to positively predict a variety of social and academic outcomes throughout childhood and into adulthood'.[6]

Positive brain connections created by 'paying attention' are there for life. When we support the development of attention skills, we create 'involved' children and establish 'intrinsic motivation', the foundation for significant and powerful learning.

Intrinsic motivation

The early childhood years are crucial for establishing robust intrinsic motivational orientations which will last a lifetime. By the time many children reach school, much of their motivation has been lost or replaced with extrinsically motivated learning strategies. Preschools and elementary schools have been criticized for contributing to such negative motivational patterns in children. This can be changed. Early childcare situations and preschools can instead be instrumental in the strengthening of children's motivation.[7]

Children are intrinsically interested and curious. They love to respond to favourite people and to their environment. They enjoy the sense of autonomy as they initiate actions and activities. They relish the sense of control. Control strengthens their feelings of competency, and this in turn leads to more exploration and curiosity. The more success they encounter, the greater the sense of competence.

Intrinsic motivation has another component, *conation*. This is the drive, the will, the determination and effort to do what we do. It is innate and powerful. Children are born with conation. A tiny baby will put all her effort into focusing on her mother's face. A three-month-old baby will concentrate hard on grabbing a toy. A ten-month-old baby will have hundreds of attempts at walking, and will go on and on trying until she can walk unaided. This is conation in action.

Somewhere during the first years of our lives, the power of conation starts to diminish. The drive to do certain things lessens. Part of this is natural; the powerful drive to walk lessens as we learn how to do it. However, there is reason to think that conation starts to decrease because of discouragement.

Discouragement impedes learning. It often leads to dropping out of school at a later stage, when a student is so disengaged that they can't see the point of continuing. When children reach that point, it is extremely hard for them to participate, learn or empathise. They are too caught up in their own negativity. Discouragement has hindered their potential to both gain enjoyment from their learning and to feel better about themselves.

Intrinsic motivation is more than an academic or developmental necessity. A motivated child is more likely to want to connect, play and relate with other children, and it is within that connection that empathy can grow. In short, motivation is crucial in order to create the learning opportunities that foster empathy.

Reliable adults

Adults hold the key to intrinsic motivation. Reliable adults create enthusiastic, interested and motivated children. *It is through our reliability that motivation is grown or restricted.*

The famous 'marshmallow test'[8] back in the 1960s showed how preschoolers who could delay gratification ended up with significant benefits later in life. They achieved better exam results, were less likely to become obese or take drugs, and consequently had improved well-being.

The test was simple. The children were given a marshmallow. They were told they could have another one if they waited for a while. They were left alone with a marshmallow while the adult left the room to 'fetch the other marshmallow'. The waiting time was fifteen minutes. Most children couldn't wait that long, some giving up straight away and pouncing on the marshmallow as soon as the adult had left the room. Others waited for a few minutes and then pounced. A few waited the whole fifteen minutes.

These same children were examined over the years as they grew into adults. It seems that the self-control elements of their childhood persisted into their adulthood.

In 2012 another study took place, which replicated the marshmallow test, but with an interesting twist; one set of children would be exposed to *unreliable* adults and experiences, and the other set would have *reliable* adults and experiences.

The 'unreliable' adult in the first set gave the child some crayons, and then promised to go and get some even better ones. The promise was not kept. The adult repeated this set of promises with stickers. Again, the child was disappointed.

The 'reliable' adult promised better crayons, and delivered them, and then offered better stickers, and delivered those.

Each group then sat the marshmallow test. The unreliable group didn't wait long for the marshmallow. What was the point? They hadn't received anything positive up to that point. The reliable group, on the other hand, waited for an average of four times longer than the unreliable group.

The 'unreliable' adults and experiences impacted the child's ability to wait, or delay gratification. Unreliable adults who say one thing, but deliver something else, are detrimental to the motivation and self-regulation of a child. An unreliable adult can be likened to a delivery service that promises next day delivery, but continually fails to do so. After a while we stop using that service. We have lost faith.

Reliable adults meet children's needs and expectations. Nothing is more powerful than an adult that promises and then delivers. We are the 'reliable' adults at our setting. Our reliability creates motivated, emotionally healthy children who trust adults because they are consistent and dependable.

Reliability is another crucial component for the foundation of empathy. When we are reliable, we demonstrate that we are thinking about the child's needs, that we are considering their perspective and that we understand their feelings.

Making sense of the world through pretend play

Pretend play begins when a young child realises that an object can 'become' something else. A toddler might 'speak' on the phone, or be 'Daddy', placing her tiny feet in Daddy's shoes. This 'symbolic' play is a significant shift from using an object literally, such as picking up a cup or hitting the floor with a toy hammer. There is a change of perspective. Objects have symbolic potential.

Through symbolic play children mimic and explore familiar behaviours – 'Naughty Teddy, go to bed NOW!' – along with past ordeals – 'Get in the car, we'll go without you' or familiar scenarios from home – 'Time for tea.'

A child's understanding of their world is called a 'working theory'. This is the accumulated understanding a child will have as they make sense of everything around them.

Children begin to own the ideas and beliefs of their culture and begin to make sense of their worlds through interactions and activities.[9]

When children play, think, observe and listen they create valuable working theories. These form their fundamental understanding of their world. Pretend play is an ideal forum.

A child's world is understandably limited. Family, friends, school, neighbours, clubs and places of worship form part of the child's circle, but beyond this the child will have little or no knowledge. Practitioners need to find out about the child's world and replicate those places. If a child has been to a café, provide café material. If another child has been to the theatre, make a stage.

There is no point in creating role-play corners that do not resonate with the children's interests. Find out these interests, diverse as they may be, and set them up as role-play opportunities. As well as exploring the familiar in their working theory of the world, children need to explore the fantastical…

For example, in our setting a few summers ago, there was a huge interest in superheroes and princesses. We created superhero costumes for the children to wear, along with princess and prince costumes. We brought in huge cardboard boxes to make castles. The children were allowed to play 'superhero' games.

Was this mirroring the real world? Absolutely not! This was a dive into fantasy…with the children making 'sense' of their observations of these 'fantastic' characters. For some it was a huge lesson in how limited they are compared with the superheroes they so adored.

But we showed them other ways of being 'super'. We applauded how fast they ran, and how they 'super-climbed' up to the playhouse. We praised them for their 'super-kindness' and 'super-tidying up'. When a child fell over, a 'super-doctor' would make them better. The potential limited nature of the superhero role-play ended up teaching the children valuable lessons about kindness and tolerance. Empathy had a chance to grow.

Young children will make assumptions about their world. These assumptions are based on limited and partial experiences. When we scaffold that play, opening up the limits and filling in the gaps, children start to make real and valuable sense of their world. It is at this point that empathy can take hold.

How stress affects pretend play

Children are more likely to cooperate and function as part of a group when they understand the established parameters, when they have 'made sense' of the situation and when they have created healthy working theories. We cannot expect a child to cooperate if they don't understand the boundaries of their shared play. A stressed or isolated child will find these parameters difficult to grasp or accept, as their overactive stress hormones will block out logical thought, leaving them victim to feelings that may engulf and overwhelm them. Other children will not respond well to their behaviour in return and a cycle where the child is further rejected may occur, leading to further heightened stress levels.

At our setting some years ago, a child consistently wrecked other children's games by knocking down bricks, kicking at bikes and generally being what we would classify as a 'nuisance'. We spent some time observing the child and talking with his parents. It turned out that his home life was extremely stressful. As a result, he didn't have the luxury of creating healthy working theories. He was too busy surviving.

These stressful conditions were impossible to remove; a family member was in prison, and another family member had moved away. However, once we had discovered these significant traumas in the child's life, we were able to work out some home/school strategies. The child responded to our responsiveness. His stress levels reduced and he was able to access the play of the other children. The adjustment in his behaviour caused the children to accept him into the group.

As a result of this early intervention, he was able to live a relatively normal life at preschool, with stress levels at safe and manageable levels. It was remarkable to observe how quickly he was able to cooperate with his peers once his stress levels had dropped. For the first time in his life, this child was able to enjoy his friendships and join in the pretend play of his friends.

We watched as he started to make sense of his world and build healthy working theories. And from there, the roots of empathy started to unfurl, and he began to accept and help other children in the same way that they had accepted and helped him. He was learning the skills of empathy.

Using pretend play to foster empathy

How do we support children in taking the leap from just pretending to be someone else, to *feeling* for someone else? Early pretend play is significantly linked to how children understand other people and their feelings. When children get involved in pretend play, they are not only re-creating experiences, but they are also often 'being' someone else, in another 'world'.

Pretend play is the act of stepping into someone else's shoes. It is half of the empathy definition. Following on from that is the understanding of someone else's feelings and perspectives.

In order to foster empathy in pretend play, the practitioner needs to:

- connect with the child

- model empathy

- name feelings

- scaffold.

What does this look like in your setting?

Connection in pretend play

A few years ago a little boy aged three came to our setting who found it extremely difficult to settle. When his mother or father left he would cry inconsolably. His language skills were limited and it was often difficult to understand what he was saying. The setting was reading a book called *Naughty Bus* by Jan Oke.[10] For whatever reason, this book captured the imagination of this boy. Each morning we would have a little toy bus waiting for him, and his key person would play alongside him as he settled into the morning. 'Naughty bus, naughty bus,' he would say, driving his little toy bus round the carpet, under the tables or over the rail track of the Brio set. It delighted him. And within his pretend play, his key person was able to offer him all the *connection* he required. They would sit together playing with the toy buses on the road carpet, or they would go outside, a toy bus clutched in his hand. They put the buses through a 'bus wash'. They dressed up as bus conductors, and issued bus tickets to anyone who wanted to get on their 'bus'.

It was this connection that gave the child confidence to come to preschool. He knew that when he arrived, he would find his bus. He knew that someone would be there to play with him and keep him company. Gradually, he started to play with other children and he moved away from his key person's side. Imagine our delight when one day he greeted another little child, crying and unhappy to leave his mother, with a 'naughty bus' for him to play with. He had learned through our modelling of how to comfort. Children see us being successful in connecting with and comforting them. They will try the same thing with others.

Connection is the foundation to all empathetic behaviour. Unless we have it, we won't model it. Our first and foremost job as practitioners is to ensure that every child in our setting feels connected. Then our work can begin.

Modelling empathy in pretend play

Children are the greatest of mimics. When we 'model' empathy to children, they will copy us. They will learn what empathy 'looks like'.

Pretend play is the perfect opportunity to model a host of behaviours: empathy, patience, kindness, turn-taking and sharing. Too often, we hover on the outskirts of children's play. It is when we adults enter into the realm of pretend play that the advantages and benefits of pretend play intensify. We literally take it to another level.

This is especially true of modelling empathy.

Some years back we had a little child at our setting who found it very hard to rein in their anger, and would stamp his feet, scream or lash out. This was scary for everyone, as well as for the child. Our plan to help was twofold. We needed to keep the other children safe while reducing the anger levels in the child.

Our first call was to model empathy. It was extraordinary to see how effective this was. Here is a typical conversation with the child.

Child: (screaming and lashing out)

Adult: (crouching down, eye contact with child, calm voice) _____ (use name of child), I can see that you are cross. Your face is cross and you are making cross noises.

Child: (calming almost immediately but continues to cry)

Adult: Let's wait a minute while that big feeling goes away. (smiles) Big feelings are not nice. It will go in a minute. (continues to wait, eye contact, touches child gently on the arm)

Child: (continues to cry, but starts eye contact with adult)

This very short conversation had the power to cut right through to the heart of the child. The adult told him that she knew he was experiencing a big feeling and that it was not pleasant. She acknowledged and labelled the feeling. She assured him that she would wait while the 'big feeling' went away. She legitimised the feeling, letting the child feel ok about being cross. The adult was making empathy 'visible'. She made eye contact with the child, she touched, she smiled and she used a calm voice. She was the essence of empathy. When a child is faced with a solid presence of empathy, she will often feel safe enough to share how she is feeling. Once a feeling is shared, its power is drastically reduced. As practitioners, we know how feelings can flare in a setting. We see it all the time. Crouching down and 'covering' a child with empathy is powerful.

Modelling empathy has a two-fold effect. It calms and it connects. These two components provide a safe space for the feeling to be acknowledged, reduce the intensity of the feeling and build up vital trust between the child and the practitioner.

Naming feelings in pretend play

How many times have you felt unsettled without understanding why? It can take time to work out our feelings, even as adults. Tiredness and stress often get in the way. Children, with their unsophisticated language skills, have an even more difficult time. When we help a child to name how they are feeling at the exact time they are feeling it, the child's stress levels begin to decrease. This feeling is similar to ours when we go to the doctor and he tells us what we need to do to get better. We feel relief, and we trust that the doctor can help us to solve our problem.

As adults, we have enough understanding of our own feelings to work out how someone else might be feeling. Very young children do not have sufficient understanding of their own feelings to be able to offer the best emotional solutions to another child. Their perspective is limited and restricted, and they have not yet learned the names for all of the feelings they are beginning to experience. The 'feeling' world can seem huge and scary.

Our job as practitioners is to name feelings for the children. Imagine one child trying to comfort another. He gives the child a teddy. Now is the time to name feelings. We can say, 'He is sad. He likes the teddy you are giving him. I think it may make him feel better.'

These words have a powerful effect. Both children are told what the feeling is, and that the kindness of the action is making a difference. Both feel validated. As we carry out this kind of scenario time after time, day after day, we may feel we are repeating ourselves. We are! This repetition builds up a child's knowledge of what feelings 'look like', what actions may help others, and what it feels like to connect with another person. It is empathy in action.

Scaffolding in pretend play

I can remember a young child at our setting who was immensely interested in fish and loved visiting the local aquarium. His key person spoke with his parents and found out that the child was able to recognise most fish, and had tanks full of them at home. How could this interest be supported, and how on earth does one bring fish into role-play?

In the end, the water tray was loaded with different types of play fish, and made more interesting by adding seaweed. We created a pretend river, where we 'fished' with real fishing rods, without any sharp bits!

This particular child found it difficult to share, and to take turns. He would become very agitated if he was unable to access a toy immediately. It was within the confines of this 'fish-based' play that he learned about sharing. His peers admired his 'knowledge'. He became the expert, and with that, he could afford to be generous with the resources: 'This is a basking shark, he has no teeth. Look.'

Where is the empathy in all of this? It is in the connections that he made. Through such play, he connected to other children and to the staff. In short, he made friends. The tiny shoots of empathy began to take shape. He started to see that other people were interesting and sometimes fun to be with. He began to see that the other children wanted to know what he knew...wanted to understand his perspective...he felt validated. As his connections grew with other children, his social 'issues' gradually faded.

When children are submerged in stimulating pretend play, creativity increases, language grows and emotional and social skills expand. This wonderful play 'status' is rarely achieved without adult scaffolding and interaction.

When we scaffold children in pretend play, we need to be as intentional as if we were teaching maths or literacy. Ideally pretend play needs to be *child initiated, adult supported and co-lived.*

When we join in, sitting on chairs jammed into the role corner kitchen, stirring 'soup' and sipping 'tea', we simply carry on the play that the children have initiated. However, we can add colour, depth and intensity to that play. We can add flavour and fun. After all, we have a vast array of experiences to place into that 'kitchen'. Take the play to a new level. Introduce an element that surprises them:

'I've found a shopping bag from the supermarket. Who wants to see what's inside?'

Let the children have the luxury of opening the bag, finding something exciting inside. Join them in bringing that play to a new level, and then retreat again. Watch them as they take on your new perspective, immersing themselves in the raised level of the pretend play. This is scaffolding in action. Watch the language grow and the ideas flow. And when they need you to help with a conflict or problem, join them, modelling empathy and connection.

Conclusion

Pretend play is packed with possibilities, opportunities and potential. It is the greatest of 'open-ended' activities. Our job is to liberate children with flexible and inspiring resources and materials, and to allow them to abandon themselves to the process of pretend play.

Deep inside this process, children learn about themselves and each other; they 'cope' with struggles, tasks and issues. They allow others to go first; they share the resources and grapple with the emerging cooperation of the group. They apply their version of 'rules'. It is, quite simply, the best of all backdrops to empathetic learning. Crucially, it is 'rooted in their [the children's] unique experience of people and events'.[11]

Deliver this powerful empathy tool in your setting. Don't have just one role-play area, have many! Have them inside and outside. Fill them with inspiring props and materials. Follow the children's interests and passions.

For a child, it is in the simplicity of play that the complexity of life is sorted like puzzle pieces joined together to make sense of the world.[12]

Pretend play is a beautiful balance of simplicity and complexity, creating the perfect forum for making sense of everything a child sees, hears and touches. Children who immerse themselves in pretend play are putting themselves in different roles and situations, trying on other 'shoes' and 'lives'. Within the peaceful parameters of pretend play, a child can exercise attention and focus, begin to name feelings, build a working theory of their world and develop the capacity to connect – all foundational components in the building of empathy.

Notes

1. Goldstein, T. (2015) How Can Children's Imaginative Play Develop Character? Big Questions Online, 17 March. Accessed on 27/06/2017 at https://www.bigquestionsonline.com/2015/03/17/how-can-childrens-imaginative-play-develop-character.
2. Smilansky, S. (1968) *The Effects of Sociodramatic Play on Disadvantaged Preschool Children.* New York: Wiley.
3. Mundy, P. and Newell, L. (2007) 'Attention, joint attention, and social cognition.' *Current Directions in Psychological Science 16*, 5, 269–274. p.269.
4. Metcalfe, J. and Terrace, H.S. (2013) *Agency and Joint Attention.* Oxford: Oxford University Press.
5. Csikszentmihalyi, M. (1990) *Flow: The Psychology of Optimal Experience.* New York: Harper and Row, p.3.
6. McClelland, M.M., Acock, A.C., Piccinin, A., Rhea, S.A. and Stallings, M.C. (2013) 'Relations between preschool attention span-persistence and age 25 educational outcomes.' *Early Childhood Research Quarterly 28*, 2, 314–324, p.318.
7. Carlton, M.P. and Winsler, A. (1998) 'Fostering intrinsic motivation in early childhood classrooms.' *Early Childhood Education Journal, 25*, 3, p.159. Used by kind permission of Springer.
8. Mischel, W. and Ebbesen, E.B. (1970) 'Attention in delay of gratification.' *Journal of Personality and Social Psychology 16*, 2, 329–337.
9. Rogoff, B. (2003) *The Cultural Nature of Human Development.* Oxford & New York: Oxford University Press, p.282.
10. Oke, J. and Oke, J. (2004) *Naughty Bus.* Budleigh Salterton: Knowall Publishing.
11. Linn, S. (2009) *The Case for Make Believe: Saving Play in a Commercialized World,* reprinted edition. New York: The New Press, p.11.
12. Knost, L.R. (2013) *Two Thousand Kisses a Day: Gentle Parenting Through the Ages and Stages.* Little Heart Books, LLC.

CHAPTER NINE

Fostering Empathy through the Process of Narrative

Helen Lumgair

Imagining what it's like to be someone other than yourself is at the core of our humanity. It is the essence of compassion. And it is the beginning of morality.[1]

Life is made up of stories. From the time we are old enough to understand, we hear stories about our parents and family members – and who we are in relation to these significant others – and this forms our sense of identity and is the beginning of our own narrative, the individual narrative. We hear about the people in our community, and further still, we hear about the people who make up our society, our nation and the wider world. This is what I will refer to as the collective narrative. All of this information is relayed through the telling of stories – either verbally, or through books, theatre, film, photographs and a variety of other mediums.

History is story. We learn of those who lived long ago, seeing through their eyes and understanding their stories. News is story. Almost all conversation is based on our own stories or the stories of those around us. These stories are endlessly discussed, as we constantly strive to make sense of the human experience. We find similarities and differences between our lives and the lives of others, thereby enhancing our sense of belonging as a citizen of the world and as a part of the global human family.

Peter Gray (2014), the eminent psychologist, says about narrative, 'Attraction to stories is basic to human nature... Stories describe the basic conflicts and dilemmas of human life and stimulate us to think about ways of resolving them.'[2] Michael Rosen, the British children's book author, sees story as a key part of the foundation of children's learning. He says, 'At the core of narrative is feeling, it is story that makes us care and pay attention and question.'[3]

Narrative encourages us to feel deeply and, at times, to take action. In my experience, the stories that are most effective are those that strive to emphasise the humanity of the characters involved and the universal experiences that people share. Such stories aim to link people together through the recognition of familiar feelings, thoughts, actions and struggles – and this allows us to begin to see others as similar to ourselves.

> The stories that attract us most are about social interactions. In one recent series of experiments, children as young as four years old showed a clear preference for stories about people or people-like animals over stories about actual animals or objects. They also preferred stories in which the protagonists had certain desires or goals they were striving for, or problems to overcome; and they preferred stories about two or more people interacting over stories about one person's solo activity. We are hungry to learn about the various harmful and helpful ways that people interact with one another, perhaps because that is what we must learn for a satisfying life.[4]

The stories we tell provide a safe space for children to grapple with the complexity of issues that they are only just beginning to understand.

> *Stories provide a simplified simulation world that helps us make sense of and learn to navigate our complex real world.*[5]

We see then that narrative can be used to equip children with a myriad of skills. The list below is not exhaustive but demonstrates what an effective tool narrative is in terms of teaching.

Through stories, children learn to:

- identify, define and re-define beginnings, middles and endings

- understand perspectives that differ from their own

- visualise and imagine a story through the eyes of different characters

- identify emotions and emotional themes

- identify with both the emotional and experiential journey of characters, and empathise with them

- make global connections

- honour differences and celebrate similarities

- gain an awareness of people in the wider world

- begin to see others as individuals with personal stories, not merely as groups of people

- seek alternative endings through collaboration, analysis and discussion considering cause and effect

- analyse the past and challenge the limitations imposed by history including gender bias, prejudice, stereotypes, racial and/or religious discrimination

- create the future, by beginning to model modified behaviour in order to present an optimistic alternative to their wider community.

It is within this rich process of narrative that we can find powerful ways of fostering empathy in the lives of children. Many psychologists understand empathy to be the very foundation of our moral compass: 'Empathy is believed...to be the biological foundation for morality. To empathize is to see the world, to some degree, from another person's point of view and to experience, at least partly, what that person is experiencing.'[6]

As we have read in Chapter 2, empathy is made up of two parts: affective and cognitive empathy. The affective part of empathy is the 'feeling', the emotional response to emotions and emotional situations. The cognitive part is the 'thinking' that enables a child to identify feelings and understand different perspectives. Narrative encompasses both of these areas, providing children with opportunities to make sense of the minds and feelings of others.

Through the processes of narrative, children begin to make personal connections. They begin to identify with characters, and to understand those characters' motives, thoughts, ideas and dreams. Vitally, narrative encourages an awareness of the self. It is through the child's own unique responses to these different narratives that feelings are born and examined. Crucially, it is an understanding of the child's own feelings that gives rise to an understanding of the feelings of others.

In order to effectively foster empathy in the lives of children, we need to focus on a few key principles.

What stories are we telling our children?

Empathy is effectively fostered in the lives of children when we choose appropriate stories. Stories can be wasted opportunities or they can be powerful ways to connect with other people. Story time is when children can begin to glimpse what other lives look like. Sue Palmer of The Empathy Lab in the United Kingdom says, 'It's not merely the ability to read that matters. It's how and what and why we read. Literature allows us to lock minds with other people from every age and background, helping us to understand not just what they think, but how they feel.'

In order to provide the best possible opportunities for the use of stories, we need to look at the type of stories we read. For this we must consider the following:

1. Can the children relate to the story and build on their existing knowledge?

2. Does the story mirror the experiences of the children in some way?

3. Does the story provide the children with rich insights into the identities and experiences of those people whose lives are different to their own?

4. What voices does the story include? Think about race, ethnicity, class, ability, religion, place, age, immigration status or socio-economic status.

5. Does the story accurately reflect real experiences in terms of characters, settings, problems and solutions through its language and illustrations?

6. Does the story promote equality and inclusion?

7. Does the content of the story perpetuate stereotypes, generalisations or misrepresentations of any kind?

8. Does the story promote justice, developing an awareness of prejudice or injustice?

9. Does the story promote action, developing the virtues of kindness and compassion, encouraging an awareness of rights and responsibilities, along with the ability to speak out against injustice and resolve conflicts?

10. Does the story promote peace, developing the desire to live in peace with others?

Of course, not every story will contain all of these elements. Nevertheless, it is a good idea to consider all stories in light of this list, as this ensures that all stories chosen are of a high quality, providing numerous rich links for exploration and learning.

How do we tell stories?

Factors to consider when telling stories:

- Do we use a monotone voice or do we bring the book alive with plenty of animation, anticipation and excitement?

- How do we direct the children's attention as we read the story? Do we ask them questions? Do we point out the most important points or principles?

- Do we immerse ourselves in the book and inspire the children to do the same?

- Is it a reciprocal process – a back and forth between the reader and the child? (By this I mean is the story 'shared, felt, or shown by both sides'?)

- Do we give the children time and space to respond to the book, to enjoy it? Are we giving children time to turn back the page and look again at the picture/s?

- Do we allow the children to laugh, to comment and to contribute their thoughts, ideas or feelings? Do we allow them to link the concepts in the book to knowledge they might already have?

Empathy is fostered through the process of telling stories when we do the following:

- Use our voices. Our voice is a powerful tool. Modulate your voice as you read or tell a story, express intense emotions by squealing with excitement or by laughing hysterically.

- Match your voice to the emotions in the story as you bring it to life. Ask questions quizzically, for example, 'Is it *really* the grandmother who's in the bed?' (Little Red Riding Hood). 'Whatever *will* the giant wear if he gives away all of his clothes?' (Julia Donaldson's *The Smartest Giant in Town*).

Draw the children's attention to the emotional responses of the characters

- Ask the children about the emotional reactions of the characters to the situations these characters find themselves in. Ask how they might feel.

- How do the children know that the character feels this way? What is it that tells them this? Where are they looking for the clues?

Focus on the emotional responses of the child and link these to the responses of the character

- Ask the children how they would feel in the same situation. Would they feel the same or would they feel something different?

- How would they react? Would they react the same or would they react differently?

- What does the book/story make them feel? And what does it make them want to do?

Focus on the thinking of the child and encourage further thinking about the story

- Time and space should be given to the children in order for them to reflect. There are no right or wrong answers. This is simply a time to encourage their thinking processes.

- For example, 'Imagine you are _____. What might you feel like sitting out in the cold?' 'What might he/she be thinking?' 'What do you think she/he is feeling?'

Engage the children in further examination of the story

- Consider whether the children have missed anything in the story.

- Have they thought about the underlying motives of the characters? Have they realised that things aren't really as they appear in the story? Work through this exploration with them, verbalising your reasoning as you proceed. This will teach the children how to approach narrative texts using critical thinking skills.

Flip the story and anticipate different outcomes with the children

- Ask the children to think about better ways, or better actions for the characters.

- Hypothesise with the children: 'What would have happened if…? And then…?' Keep this simple, using one different action and a clear resulting outcome. In this way, they will learn to consider alternative perspectives, endings and ideas. 'We will not have the capacity to solve intractable social problems, unless we have a citizenry that is capable of understanding multiple perspectives and acting on them.'[7]

Are we focusing on all three stages of narrative?

The process of narrative can be divided into three different stages – input, elaboration and output. It is vital that children experience all three of these stages, allowing them to:

- **learn about a story** and its content (INPUT)

- **consider and process the story** and its message (ELABORATION)

- **express their ideas about the story** and the learning contained within it (OUTPUT).

Narrative input

This is the stage where the children receive information presented in narrative form.

> *Stories help children make sense of their world by engaging their feelings, exploring complicated feelings and emotions, or connecting them to childhood memories through their association with characters and illustrations in picture books.*[8]

Stories can be told verbally, for example, through a simple personal anecdote recounted by the teacher. Stories can be read, using picture books, or when the children are older, text-based books. Stories can also be presented as poems or drama, using role-play, dance or song.

Narrative elaboration

This is the stage where the children elaborate on and process information presented in narrative form. The most effective elaboration for young children is experiential. The late educator Bev Bos said, 'If it hasn't been in the hand, the body and the heart it can't be in the brain!' By immersing themselves in experiential learning extending directly from a story, children are able to truly examine the content of the story, and to work through it. This is called 'Living the Story'.[9]

Children reflect on the story during circle time, small group discussions or through one-to-one interaction with the teacher. They are able to discuss, debate, anticipate and hypothesise about alternative endings. They create artwork based on the story; they play with objects from the story and they role-play using characters from the story. They act, sing and dance.

Lovegreen and Lumgair (2015) explain the rich social and emotional learning that occurs through the merging of narrative and play thus:

> It is through play that we take what we know, what we hear, what we and those close to us experience, and add it to our story. There is thinking involved. We see the cause and effect of our decisions. There is feeling involved. We feel the emotional responses of our decisions. Whether it is the exploratory play of an infant, the parallel play of toddlers, the cooperative play of preschoolers, or the intricate play of young children, both thinking and emotions are the main characters in the powerful processes of story and play.[10]

Burke believes that when a child's learning is centered in narrative, this gives the child agency: 'Stories act as a narrative web, bringing meaning and understanding about the world to children.'[11]

Children then assimilate this information, using these narratives and this new information in their play to further construct their own narratives. The stories and language used in the environment are of utmost importance because together they assist children in developing personal narratives that are emotionally literate, grounded in a sense of justice and compassion for others and reflective of diversity.[12]

Children generally develop their perspectives on aspects of identity such as gender and race before the age of five. It is therefore crucial that we choose effective stories with strong moral messages with which to work. The language that children hear in stories, in their interactions with others and in their immediate environment informs both the content of their thinking – their knowledge – and their thinking processes: 'Stories help children develop empathy and cultivate imaginative and divergent thinking – that is, thinking that generates a range of possible ideas and/or solutions around story events, rather than looking for single or literal responses.'[13]

It is vital that we constantly consider what sort of narrative and language we are providing for children as they develop intellectually. Will their internal voice be fair and just? Will it be compassionate and kind? Will it be positive and hopeful? *What will their personal narrative, aided by their thought processes, sound like?*

How do we elaborate on narrative with the children effectively? We do so by creating a safe space for children and their ideas by considering the following:

Value children's answers

Value whatever it is that children volunteer and allow them to explore their ideas, inviting them to elaborate, for example, 'I'd really like to know more about this thought or idea you've had. Could you tell me more?' Remember that no idea or suggestion is 'wrong'. As children learn that all answers are valued, their confidence will grow and their involvement in the narrative process will increase.

Remove any sense of expectation/pressure

Let children engage with the storytelling processes at their own pace and observe for as long as they need to. Often children will join in with actions and sounds, and build up to offering ideas. This is to be expected. Allow children the space and time to generate ideas, build confidence and express their ideas when they are ready to do so.

Take every opportunity to draw attention to the feelings inherent in the story

When carrying out narrative processes, talk about the feelings of the characters, for example, 'the fox seems angry', 'the girl seems sad'. By using appropriate facial expressions, emotion words and acting out these feelings, the children will begin to develop an 'emotions vocabulary' and to use accurate language in terms of their feelings.

Step back at times and let the children lead the elaboration process

The teacher's role is to facilitate the children's feedback on stories. Allow them to volunteer their own thoughts, feelings and ideas when they are ready. It is of utmost importance that the children are given agency in terms of time to reflect on stories and to communicate their ideas.

Add thinking

The teacher's role is to run with the children's thoughts and to verbalise this thinking process, adding the appropriate language and reasoning. Such scaffolding, known as *sustained shared thinking*, is key in the process of understanding. Thinking together can be facilitated by:

- re-capping on what children have said, for example, 'So you think that...'

- identifying with what the children have said, for example, 'Oh yes, that has happened to me too. One day...'

- clarifying ideas, for example, 'Am I right in thinking that if...then...?'

- suggesting ideas, for example, 'Should we possibly try it this way and see what happens?'

- reminding the children of what you've already discussed/ established, for example, 'Don't forget that we said...'

- using encouragement to further thinking, for example, 'You solved that problem really well. Now what do you think we should do about...?'

- asking open-ended questions, for example, 'How did...?' 'Why does...?' 'What happens...?' 'What do you think...?' 'I wonder what would happen if...?'

Encourage social cognition

Once the children have heard or perhaps have told a story from the character's perspective, try to swap the character and the problem around. For example, 'What would happen if the big bad wolf was the "good guy" and the three little pigs were actually the problem?' In this instance, would the wolf really be bad or would the pigs be building on land without permission? This type of shift in terms of analysing a story will stimulate creative and critical thinking skills and foster further discussion. Always look to offer alternative viewpoints in order to encourage further critical/creative thinking, starting off simply at first and increasing the level of complexity as the children develop.

Allow for humorous ideas

Neuroscience research indicates strongly that laughter activates dopamine, which serves as a reward for the brain, creates a sense of euphoria, and plays a pivotal role in people's motivation.[14] Humour is also a critical skill in thought, communication and social interaction:

> Research with all age groups shows that people who initiate humor more often show greater social participation or are judged by peers to be more sociable. The conscious use of humor in this way is undoubtedly reserved for adolescents and adults, but it may be important to cultivate humor during childhood in order that it can be well-used later.[15]

Humour can be considered a form of play, with young children drawn towards it because they find it so gratifying: 'Humor, as a form of play, provides children opportunities for playful manipulation of the real world.'[16] Humour even influences children's storybook preferences with children choosing stories that are full of the comically unexpected, which creates intense curiosity and interest on the part of the child.

A good philosophy to adopt when using humour with the children in the elaboration phase of narrative is, 'As few rules as possible, and as many as necessary'. Allow the children to be funny and silly, facilitating their learning by constantly bringing them back to the social and emotional, empathy-based learning objectives.

Get actively involved in the children's ideas

Be active, use dramatic voices, model actions and join in with the children. Teachers should not steer the story in a particular direction but become involved in *enabling* the children to express their ideas, acting as a *resource and support* in aiding the creative process.[17]

Narrative output

This is the stage where the children express their thoughts on the narrative process. Narrative output involves recall, speaking, storytelling, drama, art, song and movement. This creativity and the opportunity for expression are vital to children's development, with creativity being defined as 'a dynamic process that often involves making new connections, crossing disciplines, and using metaphors and analogies'.[18]

As practitioners, we need to reflect on whether we truly allow children time and space to create stories and to communicate those stories to us – sometimes repeatedly – thereby allowing them to find their voice.

Anne Burke cites Anthony Paul Kerby (1991) who says that, 'Narratives are a primary embodiment of our understanding of the world, of experience, and ultimately of ourselves.'[19]

Burke goes on to say:

If we recognize that a child's understanding of the world is enhanced when it is mapped as a personal narrative, we are better equipped to truly listen as their story of pivotal moments is shared… Through their storytelling, children can be recognized as experts and agents in their own lives.[20]

Ken Robinson, when talking about 'Centering the Child' (2015), says:

'Children are not born into one world: they are born into two. There is the world around them: the world of other people and things that exists… There is also the world within them: the internal world of their own consciousness, which came into being when they did and exists only because they do. As human beings, we know the outer world only through our inner worlds. We perceive it through our physical senses and we conceive it through the ideas, feelings, and values that constitute our worldview. If education is to fulfill the principles of a liberal democracy, it has to help children understand both of these worlds and how deeply they affect each other.'[21]

Narrative provides children with the opportunity to safely explore the world of other people and things in far greater breadth than their immediate environment allows them. They can then link this knowledge to their inner world, the internal world of their own consciousness. The narrative output phase helps children to clarify and take ownership of new information, ideas and knowledge. It helps them to then communicate their ideas, feelings and values to the world around them. Furthermore, narrative output provides agency in terms of being able to express this to others individually or collaboratively.

Narrative output allows for vital reflection and refinement of ideas.

Nakatsu, in discussing the expression of narrative, says that:

Students, now more so than ever, *need to be telling their stories.* Students need to be put in the driver's seat when it comes to storytelling… Storytelling is an exercise in value exploration. When students tell their own stories, they reflect on the values that are important to them and what they have done or plan to do [to] live their core-values.[22]

Individual and collective narratives

A group of empathetic individual stories will result in an empathetic collective story.[23]

Narrative works on two levels. It affects individuals – with every child and person being changed by story – and this in turn affects the collective narrative of society. When we use narrative to foster empathy in the individual lives of children, we foster empathy in society at large.

As children develop, their capacity for empathy can either grow or atrophy depending on conditions… One set of conditions that may play a crucial role in the growth of empathy consists of the stories that children hear or, later, read.[24]

Fritz Breithaupt, a specialist in German literature, speaks about narrative as a 'powerful vehicle for the development of empathy because the listeners (or readers) automatically identify with one or more of the story's characters'.[25]

When children identify with characters in storybooks they 'experience vicariously…the sorrows, joys, triumphs, defeats, and ethical conflicts of the protagonist – and maybe those of the antagonist, too.'[26]

Breithaupt goes on:

Because listening or reading is mentally active but physically passive, it promotes thought and reflection that may not occur so much in real life. In real life, the drive to action, or the stress induced, or the ego defenses that are raised, may shortcut reflection. But in fiction, where we cannot alter what happens...what...we can do is feel, reflect, and think. In the process we may learn to care about people whom we might not otherwise care so much about, including people who are quite different from ourselves.[27]

This is the desired outcome of narrative. We want children to begin to picture, to understand and to empathise with a vast array of people – people of all ages, ethnicities and cultures – from those who lead lives similar to theirs to those whose lives differ vastly from their own.

Our role as teachers is to constantly work to bridge these narrative scenarios to real-life situations – to make them relevant to the children, and in doing so, nurture each child's potential for empathy.

We do this by facilitating the developing skills of perspective-taking and critical thinking alongside compassionate and empathetic actions. We address the feelings of the characters and the children, involving hearts. We address the thinking of the characters and the children, involving minds. We use language and we name feelings. We name thoughts. We name actions.

We talk through the (sometimes challenging) process of managing feelings, exploring both the struggles of the characters we read about and our own. We talk about issues, problems and conflicts and the feelings that arise as a result. We provide language for collaboration, for resolution.

We explore cause and effect, both positive and negative. And we explore themes such as diversity, equality, purpose, struggle, resilience, hope, victory, compassion and empathy.

Narrative has been used as a means of communication and teaching for thousands of years. As human beings, we are wired to listen to stories, and to tell them. Let's embrace this natural means of transferring knowledge to build empathy – one child at a time, classroom by classroom, school by school – until we begin to see empathy taking root across the globe.

Notes

1. McEwan, I. (2001) 'Only Love and then Oblivion.' *The Guardian*, 15 September. Courtesy of Guardian News and Media.
2. Gray, P. (2014) 'One more really big reason to read stories to children.' *Psychology Today*. Accessed on 27/06/2017 at https://www.psychologytoday.com/blog/freedom-learn/201410/one-more-really-big-reason-read-stories-children.
3. Michael Rosen speaking at the ENABLE Conference, November 2015 in Kensington, London.
4. Gray (2014).
5. Gray (2014).
6. Gray (2014).
7. Gordon, M. (2017) 'Rediscovering empathy.' *Roots of Empathy*. Accessed on 17/08/2017 at www.childandfamilyresearch.ie/media/unescochildandfamilyresearchcentre/documentspdf/UNESCOfinalpresentation.pdf.
8. Burke, A. (2010) *Empowering Children's Voices Through the Narrative of Drawings*. Accessed on 27/06/2017 at www.mun.ca/educ/faculty/mwatch/mwatch_sped13/Burke.pdf.
9. Garnett, H. (2016) *Think Equal Early Years Curriculum Framework*. Accessed on 22/08/2017 at www.thinkequal.com/whoweare.
10. Lovegreen, V. and Lumgair, H. (2016) *Think Equal Early Years Curriculum Framework*. Accessed on 22/08/2017 at www.thinkequal.com/whoweare.
11. Burke, A. (2010) *Empowering Children's Voices Through the Narrative of Drawings*, p.2. Accessed on 27/06/2017 at www.mun.ca/educ/faculty/mwatch/mwatch_sped13/Burke.pdf.
12. Palmer (2005).
13. Albers, P. (2016) 'Why Stories Matter for Children's Learning.' *The Conversation*, 5 January 2016. Accessed on 27/06/2017 at https://theconversation.com/why-stories-matter-for-childrens-learning-52135?sa=google&sq=why+stories+matter+in+children%27s&sr=1.
14. Bellace, M. (2011) 'How to get high naturally.' Workshop at Lynn University, Florida. 17 October.
15. Kolb, K. (1990) 'Humor is no laughing matter.' *Early Report 18*, 1. Online from the University of Minnesota, Center for Early Education and Development.
16. Kolb (1990), p.8.
17. Adapted from Kate Shelley, 2016. Accessed on 22/08/2017 at http://talestoolkit.com.
18. Robinson, K. and Aronica, L. (2015) *Creative Schools: Revolutionizing Education from the Ground Up*. London: Penguin, p.119.
19. Kerby (1991) in Burke (2010).
20. Burke (2010), p.11.
21. Robinson, K. (2015) 'Centering the Child.' In M. Glover and E. Oliver Keene (eds) *The Teacher You Want to Be: Essays about Children, Learning and Teaching*. London: Heinemann Educational Books.

22. Nakatsu, T. (2016) *How Storytelling Works in the Brain and Why we Need Stories*. Accessed on 22/08/2017 at www.gettingsmart.com/2016/01/how-storytelling-works-in-the-brain-and-why-we-need-stories.

23. Helen Lumgair, early years consultant and Education Director at Think Equal.

24. Gray (2014).

25. Gray (2014).

26. Gray (2014).

27. Gray (2014).

CHAPTER TEN

How Social Cognition Creates Engaged Children

Valerie Lovegreen

'Thinking about thinking' has to be a principal ingredient of any empowering practice of education.[1]

Now – more than ever before – society recognises the importance of social skills. Such skills require thought and consideration. Equipped with good social skills, we can behave in a way that works for our communities and societies.

Built into these social skills lies social cognition. Social cognition is an integral part of social skills, the ability to process the vast array of social information we are exposed to as we encounter and interact with others each day. The word 'cognition' translates as 'thinking'. We humans have the unique capacity to think. We reflect on our thoughts; we think about our thinking. As a result of this, we are empowered to make decisions that will benefit our lives and the lives of those around us.

Put simply, social cognition is how we process social information; it is how we acquire it, store it, and then apply it to social situations. Crucially, it is about how we interact with others and form healthy relationships.

The individual's social behaviour is not determined by the situation he or she is in; rather, it is determined by the person's perception of that situation, broadly construed to include relevant knowledge and memory, reasoning, judgement, problem-solving, and decision-making.[2]

This puts a whole new light on social skills. These skills are not about remembering to say please and thank you. They consist of a deep level understanding and knowledge of social context.

The consensus on twenty-first century learning incorporates the 'Four Cs', all born out of crucial thinking skills. These are *critical thinking, communication, collaboration* and *creativity*.[3]

- **Critical thinking:** using our thinking to solve a problem by considering all of the options and then making a practical decision.

- **Communication:** listening and speaking in turn, holding successful conversations with others.

- **Collaboration:** connecting with people and working together, both in our immediate and global community.

- **Creativity:** being innovative, using initiative and imagination to express original ideas.

Success in life involves using these skills. It is never too early to begin to nurture them, ensuring that social cognition plays its vital role in the lives of our children.

Development of social cognition

Children thrive with strong social cognition because it helps them to be active learners, ready to tackle life and contribute to society. This type of thinking starts early, at between one and two years of age and has a growth surge between ages four and six, as children's language skills improve.[4]

How does social cognition develop? Toddlers listen to us, watch others and learn to point and gesture to communicate with others in a social way. Preschoolers acquire more words and ideas. This helps them to communicate more effectively.

They may play with siblings or friends at home or they may attend a school where they interact with children. Whether they are playing alone or with others, it is the act of playing that creates their thinking. This thinking further informs them regarding the social 'rules' of their interactions – helping them to know what to do and how to play.

When children play successfully, these positive childhood interactions help to create responsible citizens and strong, powerful adults. Likewise, these interactions help to create adults who are good at making decisions, setting goals and achieving them.[5]

Early years practitioners can play a central part in this development. By understanding the concept of social cognition, we can support and guide play, allowing children to practise their thinking skills in different social situations. It is through practice and reflection, with support from others, that children's thinking skills grow, and they develop both competence and confidence for life.

Social emotions

We are emotional beings. Sometimes we know why we feel a certain way. Sometimes we don't. Sometimes we see the effect of our feelings on others. Sometimes we don't.

The first three emotions that children generally recognise are *happiness*, *sadness* and *anger*. However, the recognition of these is merely the starting point of the development of a vast number of nuanced emotions. Being able to recognise them in oneself and in other people helps us to interact more effectively. This clearly contributes to a more successful life.

We know that it is important to help children to learn to:

- understand different types of emotions

- be aware of their own emotions

- develop the ability to manage their emotions

- become aware of how their emotions affect others.

As children grow and develop, they learn to recognise a broad range of feelings. Gradually they begin to understand whether these emotions are appropriate, and they then manage and adjust them accordingly. This understanding and learning to change or regulate emotions helps children to get along with others. In other words, teaching them to be able to identify and manage their emotions leads them to control their behaviour. This ability to self-regulate not only improves social interactions, but also the capacity to learn academic skills.[6] Self-regulation also helps children to make better decisions. This significantly reduces the daily struggles of an unregulated emotional life. Furthermore, high levels of social intelligence equate to resilience in relationships, creating greater potential for happiness and fulfilment.[7]

Philosophy and the emotions of children

People not only gain understanding through reflection, but they also evaluate and alter their own thinking.[8]

Philosophers are by nature curious. So are children. Children are deeply interested in discovering and learning. This is what makes them so creative.

In the early 1970s, Matthew Lipman threw open the doors to improving children's thinking skills by teaching them philosophy. Lipman felt strongly that it was one of the best ways of improving thinking skills, using philosophy as a dialogue between two people. Philosophers wonder, ask questions, try to understand ideas and seek the truth.[9]

It is thinking that devotes itself to the improvement of thinking.[10]

What better way to help children to improve their thinking skills than by learning to wonder, question, understand and seek the truth? Philosophy does not have to be all about sophisticated vocabulary; it can be about logical discussion.[11] Once children begin to talk, they can talk to us about ideas and we can help them by showing them the logic in the conversation.

There are certain 'elements' of philosophy that educators and parents can develop to support this type of teaching. First of all, Lipman suggests that the adults need to:

- be good listeners

- learn to interpret what the children have to say

- guide the children to logical conclusions.

Crucially, adults need to 'guide' discussions rather than 'talk at' children. In this way, they allow children to 'play' with their thinking. The children's ideas can develop independently as opposed to them trying to remember what the adult says or thinks.

One of the joys of philosophy is that both adults and children can spend time reflecting on each other's thoughts and ideas. In this fast paced world, reflection seems to be a luxury that we cannot afford. Embracing the learning and teaching in philosophy gives us permission to take time to truly communicate with each other.

Another joy of philosophy is that through such dialogue, both adult and child can use information to change their minds and expand their thinking.[12] Flexibility to change thoughts, and to be more accurate at an early age, leads to greater self-confidence and increased self-esteem, as well as improved self-control.

A third joy is that when children or adults begin to think about ideas together, they start to talk with, not at each other, and thus become more connected. Children will learn to listen effectively, speak logically and honour each other's ideas, as the adult models cooperation in conversation. Together they can use these shared ideas to create new ones. And with this sharing of ideas, a community of inquiry is formed.

Using philosophy 'with' children, and not just 'for' children, benefits both children and adults through asking questions, reflecting and sharing ideas.[13] When our young children begin to use this pattern of listening, reflecting and responding, they start to develop skills that will last them a lifetime.

Facilitating the development of this type of critical thinking at an early age allows learners to understand more complex information as they move through school, college and beyond. Such children will be well prepared for later challenges in life.

Community of Inquiry

Educationists should build the capacities of the spirit of inquiry, creativity, entrepreneurial and moral leadership among students and become their role model.[14]

When children learn to enjoy talking with others at an early age, dialogue becomes second nature. Dialogue is also a powerful tool that can be used throughout their lives. Discussion will become a part of their conversations and this will have a positive impact on their future writing skills. The type of thinking that accompanies discussion helps older students to understand literature, science, history and mathematics. Crucially, discussion creates ideas that benefit society. Such thinking is the first step towards becoming a social entrepreneur, a person whose ideas help others in need.

Higher learning teachers use a concept called Community of Inquiry in their teaching. Community of Inquiry improves learning. It teaches children how to work together to answer questions and produce new ideas, and this in turn creates more learning.[15] The teacher works with the children to help them to interact, forming a 'community' that solves problems together, with children as young as three being able to think in this way. Children reflect on what others in a group have said and then respond, honouring the thoughts and opinions of each person as they work together. Great ideas are created, and when conflict occurs these young minds use their skills to solve problems that best benefit all in the community.

Community of Inquiry starts with a question, for example, 'How can we make a den?' The group answers it, by offering ideas, listening to the ideas of others and coming to a consensus that is reasonable to all involved.[16] This organised way of thinking prepares a child to handle learning situations, in the present and the future.

Through Community of Inquiry children begin to develop the ability to create partnerships. They learn to listen to others with real intent and to speak their minds in a way that others can hear and honour.

How does the practitioner act and react in a Community of Inquiry? What is their role and responsibility?[17]

1. **The environment:** The classroom should feel open, and the practitioner should be sensitive to the ideas and interests of all children. In this way, children and practitioners develop a level of respect for each other as the practitioner accepts all answers and rephrases the children's ideas. This keeps the 'community spirit', which is at the heart of a Community of Inquiry.

2. **The dialogue:** The practitioner scaffolds the children's learning by monitoring and directing the conversation with sensitivity, suggesting ideas or reframing the ideas of the children. Practitioners can offer a paraphrased response/question any relevant information/summarise or generalise this information.

3. **The children:** Some children prefer to listen and the teacher honours this behaviour through positive body language and conversation. Some children offer ideas, and the teacher accepts them without judgement. This fosters additional inquiry by promoting/expanding these ideas.

In a Community of Inquiry, everyone feels responsible for being a part of that community. Each member contributes in some way to the collective growth of the group. Every participant develops her *personal agency*. This creates stronger self-esteem and self-understanding. Consequently, the group becomes a cohesive unit, developing a *community agency*, powerfully capable of working together on their shared learning journey.

Dialogic teaching

> *Having been an educator for so many years I know that all a good teacher can do is set a context, raise questions or enter into a kind of a dialogic relationship with their students.*[18]

As adults, we spend time thinking and reflecting before we speak. This is the essence of true dialogue. In the dictionary, dialogue is described as a conversation or exchange of information between two or more people. This exchange implies that there is a back and forth movement, with both or all parties participating.

Often in teaching and parenting, the 'conversation' seems one-sided, with the adult doing all of the talking and the child 'apparently' listening. Dialogic teaching offers a different type of dialogue and a different way of teaching that benefits both child and adult. Dialogue becomes a teaching tool, where the reciprocal and collaborative exchanges mean that children can 'think' at a higher level than they would on their own.

Fisher (2007) describes dialogue as a conversation where both parties agree, disagree, ask questions and challenge each other, and where individuals learn to change their minds as additional information is processed.[19] These skills link directly to the four Cs of twenty-first-century learning deemed necessary for success in school and life as previously mentioned: critical thinking, communication, collaboration and creativity.

The benefits for such dialogue in teaching go beyond traditional academic subjects and include improved social skills, language skills, attention, motivation and problem solving.[20] In dialogic teaching, everyone involved in the conversation begins to develop an understanding of each other, with teachers connecting with children and children connecting with teachers.

Dialogic teaching relies on speaking and listening. *These two skills together are instrumental in developing intelligence.*[21] Children share their thoughts and their emotions and in so doing, form relationships.[22] It is a two-way street, a safe environment where children feel free to speak, share and make mistakes, gradually becoming aware from their successes and their errors of what they are learning. Both children and adults work together, understanding each other's ideas, ever learning and growing.

Through sensitive questioning and commenting, a practitioner learns about the children and contributes to the development of their moral compass. Crucially, children learn to understand their own thinking.

Many educational systems today seem to focus on academics, trying valiantly to improve test scores and the memorisation of facts, rather than improving and expanding critical thinking skills. The beauty of dialogic teaching is that it supports a child spiritually, socially, morally and culturally. The focus is on stimulating thinking, making connections and sharing ideas and impressions.[23] Such teaching is a perfect platform for fostering morals and values and it points to a hopeful future, where the child learns to strengthen or even change their thoughts and beliefs.

Successful dialogic teaching

In today's society, research says that dialogue and dialogic teaching are not natural skills for adults. As a result it tends not to take place in homes and classrooms. Adults tend to 'monologue' when sharing information, with children shouldering the responsibility for listening only. Without the back and forth of sharing information, adults lose the capacity to listen, and children do not develop the ability to speak.

In addition, when dialogue is absent, children do not learn to hear the thoughts of another person. It is through the reflections and opinions of others that children grow intellectually and ultimately develop the skills needed for empathy.

Children benefit from experiencing three types of questions:[24]

What do I say?	Child speaks, thinks and responds according to their understanding
What do you say?	Child listens, considers and responds according to their understanding
What do others say?	Everyone listens, considers and responds according to their understanding

Practitioners can use this framework as a guide when starting to use dialogic teaching practices. Children develop the ability to compare their responses and this increases the complexity and abstraction of language skills.

When exposed to this type of questioning, children collect more information, learn to compare, and discover the perspectives of others. Such thinking supports the development of empathy, so vital in successful living.

There are three skills necessary for successful dialogic teaching:[25]

1. **Self-critique:** The practitioner must be aware of her thoughts and speech, and model making mistakes and learning from them. In this way, she helps children to learn from their mistakes.

2. **Narrative capacity:** In dialogic teaching, the interaction between the practitioner and the children is a story being 'constructed' in real time. In other words, the practitioner learns to 'read' the inner life of children, through their non-verbal language, their gestures, their feelings, their values; this creates an understanding of where they are in their learning world, and what support they need to progress further.

3. **Seeing the big picture:** The 'big picture' is concerned with what went before and what comes after; it is never one isolated event. The practitioner has to see the big picture in the continual story of the child's life. The child's views and perspectives will change according to this bigger picture. Practitioners should create a safe space and support children's learning by valuing the child's 'present', while being appreciative of her history.

Dialogic teaching allows practitioners and children to get to know and value each other. It encourages children to understand other people's perspectives and to respond to their ideas. In this way, children work together to achieve a goal.

In dialogic teaching, everyone benefits. It encourages purposeful, reciprocal and collaborative learning. The child becomes a valued participant with a strong individual voice, rather than a 'compliant supporter of the teacher's purpose, their voice...barely acknowledged'.[26] Such a culture of investigation and dialogue creates high-level thinking and greater opportunities for deep-level learning.

Social mindsets

Anyone can sympathise with the sufferings of a friend, but it requires a very fine nature to sympathise with a friend's success.[27]

Mindsets are very much a current topic. Teachers, parents and other professionals realise the importance of developing and maintaining mindsets that will lead to successful lives. Our mindset significantly affects how we approach a challenge. Research suggests that instead of presenting challenges, hoping that a mindset will develop, teachers need to support children in developing a mindset that will achieve a challenging task or situation.[28]

Carol Dweck (2012) talks about a 'growth mindset',[29] where a person believes that she can develop her abilities if she works hard and is dedicated to the task. A 'fixed mindset' is where a person believes that her ability or talent is 'fixed'. Fostering a growth mindset at an early age can set a student up for many successes throughout her lifetime and provide her with skills to tackle the more challenging situations life may present.

Individuals with a growth mindset are more likely to create a social mindset; this is the vital capacity to think and work with others, interact with others, solve problems and learn that growth and change are possible. The capacity for such a social mindset helps preschoolers to be reciprocal, and to grow and develop in their social world.

Barragan and Dweck's work in 2014 with one- and two-year-olds showed that children learn and connect more when they experience a reciprocal or back and forth relationship with others: 'Very simple reciprocal activity elicited high degrees of altruism in 1- and 2-year-old children, whereas friendly but non-reciprocal activity did not.'[30]

For practitioners, fostering positive social mindsets in our children begins with the words we use and the actions we take. Children listen to everything we say, watch everything we do and establish ideas about the world in which they live based solely on these experiences. When we are reciprocal and reliable, using positive words, children become more resilient. It is resilience that creates growth mindsets. However, if our words limit children's actions and thinking, they will believe they are not capable and so create a fixed mindset.

Offering positive support and ideas while helping children to develop their strengths is like walking a tightrope. We want them to thrive, and we want them to be safe. Mary Jamsek (2016)[31] offers some guidelines that adults can follow for creating a growth mindset in children:

1. Set an example, where both 'errors' and 'safe risks' contribute to meaningful learning.

2. Support problem-solving experiences; guide this process so that the child not only *learns* but also realises that they have *grown* from the experience, whatever the outcome.

3. Be sure that feedback provides information on the child's *action and effort,* concretely describing *the process,* not judging its *acceptability or results.*

4. Model a growth mindset; show children that you are willing and able to make mistakes and recover from them. Explain your process of problem solving.

Chatting with children about the social/problem-solving aspects of their experiences will expand their growth mindset. When we build empathy in a setting, talking about the perspective of the 'other' is part and parcel of the solution.

With a social mindset, children learn to think and reason, while considering both their feelings and the feelings of others. 'Look at Harry, his face is sad. What happened to make him sad?' 'You and Harry both look sad. What happened to make you both feel this way?'

Children learn to problem solve when they are allowed to develop their thinking in situations that rise up out of conflict or exploration. 'You both want the blue car. What can we do?'

Fostering this type of thinking develops young learners who will be successful members of our global society, on the simple premise that they are successful members of their own small community. Social mindsets also help older children to embrace their school and social environments more efficiently. Vitally, it helps adolescents and young adults to navigate their complex social and academic worlds, setting them up for successful relationships in adulthood.

Social entrepreneurs

Greg Dees is called the 'Father of Social Entrepreneurship'.[32] He believes that the goal of social entrepreneurship is to create human beings who have passion, sharp thinking, problem-solving skills and are on a mission to tackle social problems.[33] On reflection, these are the very same skills and values that we want for all our children, both on an individual level and for the prosperity of our global community.

Our general view of entrepreneurship is setting up a new business, hoping for healthy profit. However, the characteristics of an entrepreneur describe someone who is prepared to undertake a challenging task or project and who thinks 'outside the box'. The skills of an entrepreneur include creativity, communication, critical thinking, collaboration – does this sound familiar? All are the elements of the four Cs of twenty-first-century education. We see that teaching the four Cs at an early age is also a powerful way to facilitate the creation of *social entrepreneurs*. When taught from an early age, the four Cs become a habitual way of thinking, causing the child to develop a solutions-focused mindset and allowing the child to contribute and to make a difference in our world. Teaching with social entrepreneurship in mind allows young learners to become better learners, for themselves and their community.

A social entrepreneur has empathy for others and an insight into the needs of others. Empathy, insight and passion are all vitally important attributes. Hence, when young children are equipped with empathy and sharp critical thinking skills, they can resolve conflict, solve problems and create new ideas as adults. And in doing so, they can give back to society what society has given them, which is the ultimate expression of independence and resourcefulness.

Notes

1. Bruner, J. (1996) *The Culture of Education*. Cambridge, MA: Harvard University Press, p.19.
2. Kihlstrom, J.F. (2010) *An Introduction to Social Cognition*. Berkeley, CA: University of California, p.1.
3. National Education Association (2012) *An Educator's Guide to the 'Four Cs'*. National Education Association. Accessed on 21/08/2017 at www.nea.org/assets/docs/A-Guide-to-Four-Cs.pdf.
4. Comparini, L., Douglas, E.M. and Perez, S.N. (2014) 'The development of social cognition: Preschoolers' use of mental state talk in peer conflicts.' *Early Education and Development 25*, 7.
5. Williams, P., Sheridan, S. and Sandberg, A. (2014) 'Preschool – an arena for children's learning of social and cognitive knowledge.' *Early Years 34*, 3.
6. Goleman, D. (2008) 'The secret to success.' *Education Digest: Essential Readings Condensed for Quick Review 74*, 4, 8–9.
7. Jayson, S. (2006) 'Sociability: It's all in the mind.' *Health and Behaviour, USA Today*. 24/09/2006.
8. Bandura, A. (1986) *Social Foundations of Thought and Action: A Social-Cognitive Theory*. Upper Saddle River, NJ: Prentice Hall, p.21.
9. Lipman, M. (1984) 'The cultivation of reasoning through philosophy.' *Educational Leadership 42*, 1, 51.
10. Lipman (1984), p.52.
11. Lipman (1984).
12. Lipman (1984).
13. Vansieleghem, N. and Kennedy, D. (2011) 'What is philosophy *for* children, what is philosophy *with* children–after Matthew Lipman?' *Journal of Philosophy of Education 45*, 2, 171–182.
14. A.P.J. Abdul Kalam, 1931–2015, 11th president of India.
15. Golding, C. (2015) 'The Community of Inquiry: Blending philosophical and empirical research.' *Studies in Philosophy and Education 34*, 2, 205–216.
16. Golding (2015).
17. Canuto, A.T.O. (2015) 'Reflections on theory and pedagogy of challenges in facilitating children's dialogues in the community of inquiry.' *International Journal of Whole Schooling 11*, 1, 1–15.
18. Godfrey Reggio, American film director and screenwriter.

19. Fisher, R. (2007) 'Dialogic teaching: Developing thinking and metacognition through philosophical discussion.' *Early Childhood Development and Care 177*, 6–7, 615–631.

20. Alexander, R. (2009) *Towards Dialogic Teaching: Rethinking Classroom Talk.* York: Dialogos.

21. Fisher (2007).

22. Fisher (2007).

23. English, A.R. (2016) 'Dialogic teaching and moral learning: Self-critique, narrativity, community and "blind spots".' *Journal of Philosophy of Education 50*, 2, 160–176.

24. Fisher (2007).

25. English (2016).

26. Wolfe, S. and Alexander, R.J. (2008) *Argumentation and Dialogic Teaching: Alternative Pedagogies for a Changing World.* London: Futurelab. p.1.

27. Oscar Wilde, 1854–1900, Irish playwright, novelist and poet.

28. Pawline, S. and Stanford, C. (2011) 'Preschoolers grow their brains: Shifting mindsets for greater resiliency and better problem solving.' *Young Children 66*, 5, 30–35.

29. Dweck, C. (2012) *Mindset: How You Can Fulfil Your Potential.* New York: Random House.

30. Barragan, R.C. and Dweck, C.S. (2014) 'Rethinking natural altruism: Simple reciprocal interactions trigger children's benevolence.' *Proceedings of the National Academy of Sciences of the United States of America 111*, 48, 17071–17074.

31. Jamsek, M. (2016) 'Ask TYC: Growth mindset in preschool.' *Teaching Young Children* 10, 2, 31–33.

32. Worsham, E.L. (2012) 'Reflections and insights on teaching social entrepreneurship: An interview with Greg Dees.' *Academy of Management Learning & Education 11*, 3, 442–454.

33. Dees, G. (2001 [1998]) 'The meaning of "social entrepreneurship".' Accessed on 27/06/2017 at https://entrepreneurship.duke.edu/news-item/the-meaning-of-social-entrepreneurship.

CHAPTER ELEVEN

Empathy and Autism

I've heard too many tragic stories of the mistreatment and mishandling of autistics due to lack of knowledge. It breaks my heart because I know no one is truly at fault.[1]

These are the words of a non-speaking, severely autistic 16-year-old boy, Jordy. Having had no speech for his entire life, his therapist encouraged him to write a letter, using his right index finger, one key at a time, to explain his condition to 'neurotypicals' (people without autism). He went on to write:

With your attention, I can help you recognise the signs of nonspeaking autism. If you can recognise the signs, then you will be able to recognise our difference, which then leads to the understanding of those differences, which brings us to the wonders of acceptance. With these simple ingredients, together we can create a safe, welcoming and happy environment for both autistics and neurotypicals alike.[2]

Jordy highlights a crucial point here; *he sees how those with and without autism can create an environment together.* He sees how empathy can play its vital role of connection. He knows all too well how ignorance and misunderstanding can generate division, despite a rising awareness of Autistic Spectrum Condition (ASC). This is a condition that isolates. With empathy, we can learn to understand. With empathy, we reverse this disconnection.

Over half a million people in the UK have autism. If you count the families involved, this means that up to *three million people* are affected. That is 5 per cent of the population. Many tens of thousands of cases of autism are mild. Others are severe. The rest of them lie somewhere in between, a vast range of diagnosis. Whatever the severity, parents are dealing with a new and bewildering condition, and a 'minefield of diagnoses' or no diagnosis at all.[3] 'It was the most protracted and painful experience of my life,' says one parent from Brighton and Hove area. 'It takes too long from beginning to end,' says another. On top of this, every child with ASC faces a wide range of challenges, both on a personal and a practical level.

Seventeen per cent of autistic children have been suspended from school, with almost half of these having multiple suspensions.[4] After leaving school, 70 per cent of adults with autism feel isolated[5] and only 15 per cent of autistic adults hold down a full time job.[6] The cost of autism for each individual over an entire lifetime can be up to £2.2 million. 'Lost productivity and adult care' make up the largest part of the expense.

Once they have the diagnosis, many families of children with ASC overlook the support they need for themselves. In addition, parents of children with ASC will have different ways of coping and processing the journey. Fathers of sons with ASC may find it particularly difficult. We don't want these parents merely to 'manage', 'cope' or 'survive'. We want them to thrive, and to flourish. 'People thrive with support and understanding and feel diminished without it.'[7]

Families with children with ASC can often feel judged and belittled. Dr Temple Grandin (educator, scientist and autism advocate) was autistic and non-speaking until she was four. She had this to say about 'normal people' and empathy:

> Normal people have an incredible lack of empathy. They have good emotional empathy but they don't have much empathy for the autistic kid who is screaming at the baseball game

because he can't stand the sensory overload. Or the autistic kid having a meltdown in the school cafeteria because there's too much stimulation.[8]

Temple Grandin had people in her life that didn't give up on her: her mother, her speech therapist, and a nanny who would spend hours and hours per day playing turn-taking games with her. Empathy was planted firmly into her relationships and her play. As a result, she flourished.

A 'misfit' often isn't the problem. It is the rest of us. Our lack of knowledge prevents us from understanding. As the well-known slogan says, 'Autism is not a tragedy. Ignorance is the tragedy.' Practitioners need to learn about the condition and familiarise themselves with the disorders' challenges.

> The one common denominator for all of the young children is that early intervention does work, and it seems to improve the prognosis.[9]

The prognosis of ASC improves significantly with high quality early intervention. *Preschools are that early intervention.* It is highly likely that any diagnosis of ASC will be recent and raw. By striving to understand the condition, and helping parents to find the best support system for the child, it is possible to make a significant and lasting difference. Kindness, warmth and empathy are crucial at this time.

History of autism

The term autism was used for the first time on 24 April 1908 by a Swiss psychiatrist named Eugen Bleuler to describe one of the four symptoms of schizophrenia. The word autism comes from the Greek word, 'autos' which means 'self'. Eugen Bleuler was referring to the withdrawal into the 'self' that such a patient might suffer.

Leo Kanner, psychiatrist, spoke about autism in 1943. He used the term 'early infantile autism' to describe several children with very similar patterns of behaviour; they all found it difficult to relate to other people, they had delayed language, they had similar repetitive types of obsessions, and all had exceptional memories for rote memory tests. He had this to say about the condition: 'There is from the start an extreme autistic aloneness that, whenever possible, disregards, ignores, or shuts out anything that comes to the child from the outside.'[10]

Kanner understood autism to be the result of a lack of maternal warmth. This was known as the 'Refrigerator Mother' theory of autism. This theory has been thoroughly disproved.

Kanner's work is still widely known, as is the work of Hans Asperger, who until 1981 was virtually unknown outside German literature. Hans Asperger, an Austrian paediatrician, used the word in its more modern sense in 1944, when he identified a pattern of behaviours and abilities with what he called 'autistic psychopathy'. This behaviour pattern showed 'a lack of empathy, little ability to form friendships, one-sided conversation, intense absorption in a special interest and clumsy movements'.[11] This set of behaviours went on to be known as Asperger's Syndrome (AS). Asperger would call children with AS 'little professors' because of the way they would talk about a subject in such great detail. He was sure that they would use this knowledge in their adulthood. He followed one particular child, called Fritz, all the way into his adulthood. Fritz became a professor of astronomy, and even discovered an error made by Isaac Newton!

During the 1950s, a psychologist named Bruno Bettleheim built on Kanner's work, also using the term 'refrigerator mothers' to describe the condition created when mothers neglected their children; he too was convinced that 'early infantile autism' was an emotional disorder due to the harm brought upon the child by such neglect, resulting in autism. This was categorically disproved in the 1960s.

Bernard Rimland, a research psychologist, argued in 1963 that autism was not related to the bond between parent and child. As the father of a child with autism, he claimed that it was actually a biological condition. These studies went largely unnoticed until a group of parents, fed up with the mother blame myth, got together, and with Rimland at the helm, founded the Autism Society of America in 1969.

It wasn't until 1981 that an article written by Lorna Wing brought Asperger's Syndrome to the attention of the English speaking world.[12] The syndrome was little known before this point. The wildly fluctuating false claims of maternal neglect had actually prevented experts from providing real support for those children with autism. Wing's paper showed how the underlying core features of autism could be more widespread than was previously thought. There followed an increased awareness of the symptoms of autism, and a huge surge of diagnoses during the 1990s and into the new millennium.

Among this surge came new fears that autism was on the rise, caused by vaccines. At the same time, scientists wondered about environmental triggers; were they playing a role in the rise in autism? The vaccine scare has never been substantiated, and new brain research is showing that while genetics strongly influence the risk for developing ASC, they do not account for all types of the condition. Environmental triggers *are* increasing the risk of autism; these include parental age at conception (older parents), preterm babies, maternal nutrition and infections during pregnancy.

However, a recent study shows that the annual incidence rate of autism seems to have plateaued and slowed over the last seven-year period. After a fivefold increase of autism in the 1990s, 'the incidence and prevalence rates in 8-year-old children reached a plateau in the early 2000s and remained steady through 2010'.[13] In the USA autism rates remained unchanged from 2010 to 2012. Clearly there is a need for several successive studies to confirm this deceleration of autism.

In 2013 the American Psychiatric Association (APA) published their latest manual, DSM-5, which provides the specific criteria needed to make a diagnosis of autism. For the first time the umbrella term, Autism Spectrum Disorder, had replaced all the separate terms for autism: Asperger's Disorder, Autistic Disorder, childhood disintegrative disorder and PDD-NOS (pervasive developmental disorder not otherwise specified).

This brings us to this point in time. Autism is still a relatively new and unexplored area. While much research has taken place and is underway, it remains a disorder that is largely misunderstood by the masses.

What is autism?

Autism is a condition for life. It isn't an illness, and therefore there is not a 'cure'. The spectrum on which it is based shows a varied and multi-layered number of symptoms and behaviours. This is what makes it so difficult to treat; there are thousands of variables.

Not only is autism complicated and cryptic. People also have many misconceptions about autism such as:

- People with autism cannot feel or express emotions.

  They can and do express emotions. They simply communicate them differently.

- People with autism don't have empathy.

  People with autism do have empathy. It is the communication of this empathy that is challenging for them.

- People have autism because of bad parenting.

  This theory was disproved decades ago.

Generally speaking, people with ASC will find it difficult or impossible to share their feelings, and to make friends. They won't always understand or be able to communicate what other people might be thinking or feeling. They will feel deeply, and they will communicate, but not necessarily as expected.

Philip, a young boy with ASC had this to say about it:

My eyes can see very well. Most people seem to need to have to look long and hard to make sense of a picture. I can take in a whole picture at a glance. Each day I see too many petty details. I look away to not get overwhelmed by a lot of little bits of information. I watch things that a teacher or person I listen to tells me to watch. This helps me concentrate on what I should be focusing on... I am assessing many sounds too, I have to erase some stimuli to access my answers to people's questions and meet their demands. I am sad when people think I don't like them. I love people.[14]

Such self-absorption characterises this condition, and, coupled with the social challenges children with ASC face, means that their personality can appear 'closed' to the outside world. As a result, they can appear mysterious and enigmatic. People find this challenging, preferring 'open and obvious' because it is easier to handle.

Some children with ASC will do well at school. Others won't. Some may want to take part in social activities. Others won't. Some may struggle with language. Others won't. Autism is complex. So are children with ASC. 'Each is a complicated, wondrous being'[15] with delightful ways of describing. One man called the hole in his sock 'a temporary loss of knitting'![16]

What do we do in the face of so many shifting aspects and traits?

We erase misconceptions or misunderstandings of the *disorder* by becoming familiar with it. We erase misconceptions or misunderstandings of the *child* by getting to know him. It really is that simple.

The world of the child with ASC is safe, comfortable and *his*. We should not attempt to set about changing his world but rather make it our aim to support him in it. For this, we have to educate ourselves, and gain fresh and relevant insights into the realm of the child with ASC.

Areas of autism

The three main areas of autism are social communication, social interaction and social imagination. Alongside these runs sensory processing.

Social communication and interaction skills

Anyone on the spectrum has some sort of difficulty with his *social communication skills*. These are learned and formed by practice. Most of us learn these by absorbing social cues. For example, we learn that in a library we speak very quietly and that we can shout at a football match. We cannot shout in a library.

Likewise, the back and forth of conversations can be very challenging for some children with ASC, particularly small talk with its inherent use of irony or humour. Equally, non-verbal communication, such as body language or facial expressions, can be hard to interpret.

Difficulties with *social interaction* are classic signs of a person with ASC. The child may seem bored, or remote, or else completely disinterested in the people around him. This has an effect on friendships and relationships. How hard it is to be with a person who shows no real interest in us. Of course, a child with ASC will want to make friends and be a part of the group, but may blunder his way into a conversation without the skills that the other children have. This can lead to a greater sense of isolation for the child with ASC, and reluctance to try again in such a situation.

Many children with ASC won't make eye contact. They cannot pick up on the vital cues of facial expression, body language or tone of voice. As a result, they come across as rude or disrespectful when they are neither.

Neurotypical people generally know when to smile, to shrug and to wink. We know when other people are bored, scared, angry or shy, just by glancing at their facial expression, or noticing their body language or tone of voice.

For people with autism spectrum disorders, this 'body language' can appear just as foreign as if people were speaking ancient Greek. This means that we miss out on many of the things that people are trying to convey to us and can ourselves send mixed signals when the words we use are not consistent with what our body is saying.[17]

Ignorance about ASC often starts at this point. We get offended because a child with ASC appears to be disrespectful or ill mannered, when they are neither. They simply lack these vital communication skills.

Our understanding will maintain the vital connection between the child with ASC and ourselves. *The child with ASC and their family must guide us on how best to connect.* They become the teacher, and we become the learners. It won't feel comfortable or 'normal' but it will hold the potential for opening doors into the ASC world. Understanding how an child with ASC best communicates is the first vital step along the way to knowing who they are, and what they want.

Social imagination

Social imagination is a complex skill that we largely take for granted. It helps us to understand or predict how other people behave, and to imagine the perspective of another. We are able to identify hazards and play imaginatively. This is part and parcel of the development of theory of mind, discussed in Chapter 3.

Children with ASC have poor theory of mind. They will find it difficult or impossible to understand another person's perspective, to identify danger or risk or engage in imaginative play. Sometimes it will look as though they are playing imaginatively because they will copy something they have seen, word for word, action for action. However, the newness of imaginative play, the originality of such play will escape them.

Most significantly, new situations will be challenging for their social imagination. They can't process what might happen next, because they can't imagine it. It is therefore very frightening.

Sensory processing

Our senses provide us with important information about our environment; they tell us if the environment is hot, cold or noisy. They inform us about the scratchiness of our socks or the tightness of our clothes. Sensory processing 'tunes out' or filters any unneeded sensory information. A child with ASC processes such information differently; the sensory information is exaggerated or diminished. Clothes can feel unbearably scratchy or shoes too constricted. There might be an extreme aversion to noise, sound or light.

Children with ASC consistently report hypersensitivity (high in sensitivity) or hyposensitivity (low in sensitivity) in their visual, tactile and auditory world, and there is also research that shows that their olfactory (sense of smell) is affected.[18]

> I do not see the world as others do. Most people take the routines of life and day-to-day connections for granted. The fact that they can see, hear, smell, touch and relate to others is 'normal'. For me, these things are often painfully overwhelming, non-existent or just confusing.[19]

Hyper/hypo sensitivity for a child with ASC has real implications for a setting. *We must discover and address any challenges the child may have in sensory processing.* It is rather like removing a splinter; the agitation created by a tiny splinter in our foot can make walking impossibly painful. Once the splinter is removed, we can walk again without pain.

Getting to know the child with ASC

> At times our very state as autistic individuals seems to threaten the neurotypical (non-autistic) world because we show you up for who you really are. Please don't be part of the 'us' and 'them' syndrome. Don't succumb to ignorance and typical thinking. Take the time to get to know 'autism'. Take the time to get to know us.[20]

Here is the crunch. We need to get to know the child who can't look us in the eye, or recognise that we have feelings too. We need to understand someone who finds it difficult or impossible to understand us. We need to step into his shoes and stop succumbing to ignorance. In short, we must start to empathise.

How do we communicate with a child who communicates differently to us? How do we interact with a child who finds interaction a challenge?

Here's how to do it.

Connection

> *Autism is often feared*
> *but I am not to be feared.[21]*

We start to identify the child's needs through connecting with him and with his parents/carers. Observations and assessment are part and parcel of the procedure, but it is our connection that is vital for building empathy.

Connection is active. Connection implies listening and exchanging information, ideas, feelings and thoughts. Parents of children with ASC are often tired of judgement and in need of understanding and support. Your connection with them may well be the lifeline they need.

Children with a suspected but undiagnosed disorder will have an effect on the other children and parents in the setting.

Our understanding and lack of judgement at this stage are crucial. Read the blogs and websites on autism. Every single one begs for understanding.

To gain this connection we must observe:

- **How does the child listen, how do they pay attention?** What do they understand? How do you know? How do they use words or sentences? Can they gather information or provide it?

- **How do they interact with other children**? How do they play? Who do they play with? Do they play alongside children, or with them? Is their play adult directed or child directed?

- **What are the child's special interests**? What do they love? What fires them up? What motivates them? What makes them happy to join you each day? What are their preferences? Do they prefer milk to water? Sitting on the ground or on a chair? Which toilet do they prefer? Why?

- **What are the child's fears or frustrations?** Think about the child's sensory world. What sets him off? Does the fire alarm scare him? Does the sound of the tidy up music disturb him? Does the child need a quiet place to go and recharge? Does he notice odours that no one else is aware of? Does the child find shared reading difficult? Might it be a visual processing difficulty? Many of the child's fears and frustrations will be bound up in the environment and in his capacity for sensory stimulation. Ask the child's parents. Ask the child. Find out everything. Pass it on to other members of staff.

You will slowly begin to build a picture of the child. *Keep talking, listening and being with the child.* There are no short cuts for this process. It will take as long as it takes.

The child with ASC is just a child. We must stop singling out the one glaring diagnosis (ASC) and start to find out all of the characteristics and quirks that make up this person in our care. The child is unfolding, learning and developing. Our understanding of their core challenges and how to work on those in the setting are key to the child's future happiness and success.

Physical environment

Learning how each individual autistic person's senses function is one crucial key to understanding that person. The senses of an autistic can seem too acute at some times and not acute enough other times. These particular patterns need patience to observe.[22]

I cannot stress how important it is to get the physical environment right.

We need to look at our setting's physical environment with new eyes and notice all the potential sensory challenges for our children with ASC. There will be many triggers to their sensory issues and we must avoid them where possible, both inside and outside the setting. Sensory distress is very real to children with ASC, and can be extremely unpleasant.

You can make a start with these questions:

- How crowded is the room? Does it feel cluttered or open? What looks busy and fun to you may seem chaotic to a child with ASC.

- Are there bright displays and colours everywhere? Do these seem to overload our child with ASC? Are there places that have just natural colours? *Remove clutter from notice boards. Calm the place down with more neutral colours. Wear plain, muted block-coloured clothes.*

- Is the light source natural, florescent or spotlight? Does the sun shine directly onto the playing spaces, creating a glare? *Provide a peaked cap for the child, or sunglasses. Draw the blind partially down to reduce the glare.*

- Does the setting have quiet places, a peaceful reading corner, or somewhere like a small tent or play hut where the child can go when over stimulated? Are there predictable noises or unpredictable noises? Do the florescent lights hum? How noisy is the blind when you pull it down? *Warn the child if ever there are loud noises occurring. If necessary, have some headphones available for when the child is overloaded with environmental noise.*

- Are there practitioners who speak loudly? Do they use over the top/complicated gestures? Does their tone of voice cause anxiety? *Use calm voices and simple gestures.*

- What messy play is available? Are there different types to help both children with hyper and hypo sensitivity? Does the child object to messy play? Does he find it challenging? *Explore other resources, such as sand, water, cooked spaghetti, shredded paper, shaving cream, and so on.*

- What about the general smell in the setting? What about any other smells? Are these strong? Will they affect your child with ASC? *Avoid strong perfumes or cleaning materials.*

Ask the parents/carers of children with ASC for more information from home. Keep asking. Share your findings with colleagues. Once these triggers are reduced, the child's stress levels will fall.

> There are many things that people with autism often seek to avoid: external control, disorder, chaos, noise, bright light, touch, involvement, being affected emotionally, being looked at or made to look. Unfortunately many educational environments are all about the very things that are the strongest sources of aversion.[23]

When we reduce the aversion, we increase the chances of the child's well-being and learning. We've taken that splinter out of the foot. Now the child can walk.

Reinforcement

Reinforcement is strengthening a child's skill or behaviour by providing something that motivates them to *repeat that behaviour or the skill*. Reinforcement motivates the child towards an anticipated and desirable consequence, and this in turn shapes the child's future behaviour. It is recognised as being the most effective approach in dealing with children with ASC's challenging behaviours.

We all know how hard it can be to motivate a child. I've provided a reinforcement inventory in the appendix at the end of the book, which you are welcome to download from www.jkp.com/catalogue/book/9781785921438 to print and fill in. If you complete the reinforcement inventory, with the help of the child's family, you will see very clearly what motivates your child with ASC. Add more reinforcements to the list and remove irrelevant ones.

If your child with ASC finds it difficult to leave Mum in the morning, offer his favourite racing cars to reinforce his behaviour as she leaves. If you know he likes to listen to music, use it to reinforce his behaviour when he finds a transition tricky. These 'motivators' will be life changing for the child with ASC. The child can face change without fear and can often take refuge in an activity that he values and enjoys.

Language

Is the child verbal or non-verbal? What are the child's language needs? How does he make his choices in the setting? Does he use pointing? Signing? Photos? Words?

- **Avoid any closed questions with children with ASC.** To the question, 'Did you have a nice time at the party?' the child with ASC may give you a 'yes' or 'no' answer only as this is what you have inadvertently asked for. A friend's autistic son went to a concert recently and came back thrilled and excited by the whole adventure.

He chatted non-stop about the concert once he got home. However, when a well-meaning adult asked him the next day at school, 'Did you enjoy the concert?', the boy simply said, 'Yes.' To his highly literal mind, the question had to be answered as a yes or no. And yet, when another adult asked him what he had done at the concert, he never drew breath and told them everything. The open and closed question throws up completely different dynamics; the closed question an end to the conversation, the open, the creation of it.

- **Approach the child with ASC quietly.** If you call him across the room, the chances are that he won't hear. There are so many other sounds that will drown out your voice.

- **Say one thing at a time.** The child with ASC may well find two sentences very confusing. 'Let's get your coat on and go into the garden.' He might pick up on 'coat'. The rest will be lost in a jumble of words.

- **The child with ASC generally won't get your jokes.** Jokes often have no meaning to the child with ASC because he tends to think on a concrete level and will interpret all language literally, decoding rather than inferring.

- **Look at the child's body language.** Get to know it well. When he curls up his fists is he angry or stressed? When he closes his eyes is he scared?

- **Get to know the child's particular traits.** Sometimes the child will start talking nineteen words to the dozen, because he has memorised something that his parents have said, or lines from a TV programme. This is the 'little professor' that Asperger talked about in his work. Its proper name is 'echolalia'. Often a child with ASC knows that by spurting out a whole string of words he may be able to avoid replying to you. This may be a sign of stress or pressure. No amount of chat from you will cut through his stream of words. Let him speak. Try showing him something that he loves (reinforce) and allow him time and space to relax into the reinforcement. This will reduce his stress.

- **Provide visual support.** Children with ASC need to be *shown* how to do something. Visual timetables or information are really vital for children with ASC. They miss important information because they absorb too much detail around them. Imagine a train station without a timetable. Everywhere you look people are shouting out the times of the trains, but you can't hear because of the noise and commotion. A picture timetable transforms the panic of information overload. Children with ASC can relax when they know that information is within their grasp and that they can come back to it at any time. Anxiety and frustration will dissipate.

Making choices

Making choices and decisions is particularly challenging for children with ASC and so they often avoid making them. Behind each choice lurks the apprehension and fear of getting something wrong. Early intervention can be extremely helpful in this area. Our empathetic manner renders this potentially terrifying ordeal manageable. Such choice making needs to be merged seamlessly into the day's activities: 'Would you like milk or water?' 'Shall we get the bricks or the Lego out?' 'Shall we stay outside, or shall we go back inside?'

Merge these choices into everything the child does. If he doesn't make the choice, make sure he sees that *you have made the choice for him*. Gradually he will see the consequences of not making a choice may not coincide with what he wants. Sometimes you will need to make a choice for him, for safety reasons or to avoid hurting someone's feelings: 'I'm putting your coat on now so that you keep warm.'

This vital life skill requires hundreds and hundreds of practice choices. Our quiet understanding can result in him making choices without any undue stress.

Routines

> Reality to an autistic person is a confusing, interacting mass of events, people, places, sounds and sights... Set routines, times, particular routes and rituals all help to get order into an unbearably chaotic life. Trying to keep everything the same reduces some of the terrible fear.[24]

Routines are vital to the child with ASC. The overwhelming, overloaded world is highly stressful and routines provide welcome stability and order. Your setting will have routines and these will give the child some control over his environment and help him to predict what will happen next.

However, even the smallest of transitions can be challenging for the child with ASC. We need to ease these anxieties. This is best resolved in the following ways:

- **Use visual daily timetables, or 'now and next' boards.** These will help the child to 'see' what is going to happen next. These can be displayed in a small book or folder, or on a board where the child can go and look. A single symbol, which the child can hold or put in his pocket, can alert the child to an upcoming transition, such as going outside.

- **Keep the routines predictable.** Allow plenty of time and space for the child to adjust to the next part of the routine. Never hurry the process.

- **Avoid ritualistic routines.** Sometimes routines become ritualistic, and the child starts to rely on the routine such as a particular toilet or place on the carpet. This can create a new challenge. What if the only toilet he likes to use is out of order? Prepare for all changes in advance and be aware that dependency on a routine is more marked when the child is stressed or tired.

Conclusion

Bless those who see life through a different window and those who understand their view.[25]

Working with children with ASC can be challenging. There are good and bad days. And that's OK. Keep a safe spot available at all times, especially for the particularly challenging moments. If the child needs to escape there, give them the time and space to do so. There is no linear development process here. With jumps and starts, with leaps sideways, downwards and up, the child with ASC will learn about the world outside of his. It can be painfully slow at times. That doesn't matter. The most important thing is that we keep plying ourselves with knowledge about the child and knowledge about the disorder. We can't ever know 'too much'.

Empathy grows from connection and knowledge. So, keep connecting and keep learning. The presence of our empathy in these situations is profound. We may not see an immediate difference in the child. We may sometimes even see deterioration. Whatever we observe, we must continue to connect and to learn about the child. This is because consistency and connection always works, without exception.

Empathy helps to unlock the child with ASC. Empathy helps to create a future. It is, quite simply, the link between our differences.

Take a look through their window. It's a wonderful view.

Notes

1. Itkowitz, C. (2016) 'This Nonspeaking Teenager [Jordy Baylinson] Wrote an Incredibly Profound Letter Explaining Autism.' *The Washington Post*, 19 May.
2. Itkowitz (2016).
3. See Managing Autism Spectrum Condition Ourselves Together (mASCot). Accessed on 04/09/2017 at www.asc-mascot.com/Our-ethos-and-commitment.html.
4. Reid, B. (2011) *Great Expectations.* London: The National Autistic Society, p.8.
5. Bancroft, K., Batten, A., Lambert, S. and Madders, T. (2012) *The Way We Are: Autism in 2012.* London: The National Autistic Society.
6. Redman, S., Downie, M., Rennison, R. and Batten, A. (2009) *Don't Write Me Off: Make the System Fair for People with Autism.* London: The National Autistic Society, p.8.
7. Managing Autism Spectrum Condition Online Together (mASCot) (2013) Survey of services for children with an Autistic Spectrum Condition in Brighton and Hove. Oct–Dec 2012.
8. A Conversation with Temple Grandin, National Public Radio, 20 January, 2006.
9. Autism Research Institute *Interview with Dr. Temple Grandin.* Stephen Edelson, 1 February 1996.
10. Kanner, L. (1943) 'Autistic disturbances of affective contact.' *Nervous Child* 2, 217–250.
11. Asperger, H. (1944) 'Die "Autistischen Psychopathen" im Kindesalter.' [The 'Autistic Psychopaths' in Childhood.] *Archiv für Psychiatrie und Nervenkrankheiten 117*, 73–136.
12. Wing, L. (1981). 'Asperger's syndrome: A clinical account.' *Psychological Medicine 11*, 115–129.
13. Taylor, B., Jick, H. and Maclaughlin, D. (2013) 'Prevalence and incidence rates of autism in the UK: time trend from 2004-2010 in children aged 8 years.' *BMJ Open 3*:e003219.
14. Reyes, L. (2015) 'Someone asked my son with autism why eye contact is hard. This was his answer.' Accessed on 27/06/2017 at https://themighty.com/2015/01/why-is-eye-contact-difficult-for-people-with-autism. Used with kind permission of Lisa Reyes.
15. O'Neill, J.L. (1999) *Through the Eyes of Aliens: A Book About Autistic People.* London: Jessica Kingsley Publishers.
16. Wing (1981).
17. Perks, S. (2007) *Body Language and Communication: A Guide for People with Autism Spectrum Disorders.* The National Autistic Society, p.1.
18. Ashwin, C., Chapman, E., Howells, J., Rhydderch, D., Walker, I. and Baron-Cohen, S. (2014) 'Enhanced olfactory sensitivity in autism spectrum conditions.' *Molecular Autism 5*, 53.
19. Lawson, W. (1998) 'My life as an exchange student with Asperger syndrome on an exchange programme from Monash University, Australia to the University of Bradford, England.' *Autism 2*, 290–295, p.291.

20. Bogdashina, O. (2003) (Foreword L. Lawson) *Sensory Perceptual Issues in Autism and Asperger's Syndrome: Different Sensory Experiences, Different Perceptual Worlds*. London: Jessica Kingsley Publishers.
21. Reyes, P. (2017) 'Autism is my world.' Accessed on 27/06/2017 at http://faithhopeloveautism.blogspot.co.uk.
22. O'Neill (1999), p.31.
23. Williams, D. (1996) *Autism: An Inside-Out Approach: An Innovative Look at the Mechanics of 'Autism' and Its Developmental 'Cousins'*. London: Jessica Kingsley Publishers, p.284.
24. Joliffe, T., Landsdown, R. and Robinson, C. (1992) 'Autism: A personal account.' *Communication 26*, 12–19, p.17. Used by kind permission of the National Autistic Society.
25. Author unknown.

Afterword

It is easier to build strong children than to repair broken men.[1]

Our society spends too much time and money repairing broken men, women and children. At the last count in 2010, the total global cost in lost output of work due to mental disorders was over $2.5 trillion. This amount is expected to double by 2030.[2]

It doesn't have to be this way. We now know, through a number of recent studies that have provided us with robust evidence, that the early years classroom holds the key to building 'strong' children. It is during these vital years that our children's brains become wired for their future. At no other point during their lifetime are warm and loving relationships so crucial in developing mind, body and heart.

Historically, we have left the education of children's hearts to chance. There is a very real deficit of empathy. Young adults of this generation have roughly 40 per cent less empathy than the young adults of twenty to thirty years ago.[3] Whatever the reason for this decline, the current group of students are seen as 'the most self-centred, narcissistic, competitive, confident and individualistic in recent history'.[4]

It is up to us to counteract this deficit. You, the practitioner, can make a difference. You hold the key to building strong children. The development of empathy is inhibited in an environment where indifference, negativity and stereotyping form part of the culture. However, where there is a culture of acceptance, understanding and tolerance, empathy flourishes.

Children are wired to connect with others and the human brain is designed for reciprocity – the back and forth of interaction and engagement. A child is not, however, wired for accurate, relevant and wise decisions. These are brought about by numerous experiences, where reliable adults model, support and encourage the development of empathy. These frequent learning experiences lay down the neural pathways in the brain for life.

Empathy is often viewed as just a 'heart' decision. It is not. True empathy uses the mind. It is both an emotional and thinking response. Without the vital 'thinking' element, empathy becomes its much less effective associate, sympathy.

Our personal empathy is the foundation for social empathy, 'the ability to understand people by perceiving or experiencing their life situations and as a result gain insight into structural inequalities and disparities'.[5]

Social empathy is a potent catalyst. It allows whole societies to gain an increased understanding of the issues affecting others. Once communities understand each other's perspectives, there is room for social cohesion.

Lacking a deep understanding of others can lead to scapegoating, distrust, and in extreme cases destruction of other cultures.[6]

Our role as early years educators is to raise children's awareness of themselves and others, and to provide them with the *context* for perspective taking. The very things that divide society – prejudice and stereotyping – can then be examined from an early age, creating a healthy culture of acceptance and tolerance. In this way, the positive brain connections are strengthened, and the weak ones fall away. A strong child is built.

Another key role we play is that of listener. When children are listened to they feel valued and connected. Connection is vital in terms of our healthy development. Brené Brown says this about connection:

Connection is why we're here. We are hardwired to connect with others, it's what gives purpose and meaning to our lives, and without it there's suffering.[7]

Take the example of Josh Shipp, a former foster child thrown out of every foster home he ever lived in, until he finally ended up with a foster father who refused to throw him out. The foster father saw Josh as 'an opportunity, not a problem'. He established a sound connection with Josh, for the first time in Josh's life.

This loving and empathetic connection turned Josh's life around. He went on to become a motivational speaker, and now reaches out to millions of teenagers throughout the world. His stock phrase is, 'Every kid is one caring adult away from being a success story.'

You are the caring adult. You contribute to the success story of the children in your care. Research irrefutably proves that such connection paves the way for a healthy, successful life.

Empathy matters. It breaks down shame, anxiety and fear. It overcomes division. It plants understanding and connection. It is the brain-driven, heart-compelled skill that requires a conscious choice.

Empathy is a strange and wonderful thing. It has no script. There is no right way or wrong way to do it. It's simply listening, holding space, withholding judgement, emotionally connecting, and communicating that incredibly healing message of 'You're not alone.'[8]

Your setting will maximise the effectiveness of empathy when you make supportive adult/child connections an absolute priority, when you offer hundreds of encounters and experiences for each child, where they learn about conflict resolution and self-regulation skills and when you try to the best of your ability to breathe empathy into every encounter and conversation you have.

We see how early childhood experiences are so important to lifelong outcomes, how the early environment literally becomes embedded in the brain and changes its architecture.[9]

I leave you with this. Begin today. Connect with the children. Get down on the floor and look into the eyes of the child that finds life a battle. Uncover her thoughts. Walk around in her shoes. Discover her feelings. Understand her struggles. Support her in her challenges and celebrate her successes. Walk beside her, as she becomes a participating and contributing part of the community.

If you treat an individual as he is, he will remain how he is. But if you treat him as if he were what he ought to be and could be, he will become what he ought to be and could be.[10]

We can do nothing greater than this in order to shape the lives of the children in our care.

There is an unexpected magnificence in our children and an underestimated power in their ability to change our world for the better. It is through our children that we can go beyond the frontiers of science and technology to explore the recesses of the human heart. We have managed to harness the power of the wind, the sun and the water, but have yet to appreciate the power of our children to effect social change.[11]

It all boils down to what each and every one of us does in our own small corner of the world. We can make a difference on a daily basis. And empathy is not optional. Empathy is an essential part of being fully human, the glue that binds us together in our quest for a fruitful, peaceful future for all humankind.

Notes

1. Frederick Douglass, 1818–1895, African-American abolitionist, writer, orator and statesman.
2. Bloom, D.E., Cafiero, E.T., Jané-Llopis, E., Abrahams-Gessel, S. *et al.* (2011) *The Global Economic Burden of Noncommunicable Diseases.* Geneva: World Economic Forum.
3. Konrath, S.H., O'Brien, E.H. and Hsing, C. (2010) 'Changes in dispositional empathy in American college students over time: A meta-analysis.' *Personality and Social Psychology Review 15,* 2, 180–198.
4. Alleyne, R. (2010) 'Generation me students have less empathy than 20 years ago.' *The Telegraph,* 28 May. Accessed on 21/08/2017 at www.telegraph.co.uk/news/science/7779290/Generation-me-students-have-less-empathy-than-20-years-ago.html.
5. Segal, E.A. (2016) *Social Welfare Policy and Social Programmes,* 4th edn. Boston, MA: Cengage Learning, p.1.
6. Glick, P. (2008) 'When Neighbors Blame Neighbors: Scapegoating and the Breakdown of Ethnic Relations.' In V.M. Esses and R.A. Vernon (eds) *Explaining the Breakdown of Ethnic Relations.* Malden, MA: Blackwell Publishing, p.129.
7. Brown, B. (2012) *Daring Greatly: How the Courage to Be Vulnerable Transforms the Way We Live, Love, Parent and Lead.* London: Penguin, p.8.
8. Brown (2012), p.82.
9. Andrew Garner, quoted in Gerwin, C. (2013) *Tackling Toxic: Stress Paediatricians Take on Toxic Stress.* Center on the Developing Child, Harvard University. Accessed on 4/7/2017 at http://developingchild.harvard.edu/science/key-concepts/toxic-stress/tackling-toxic-stress/pediatricians-take-on-toxic-stress.
10. Johann Wolfgang von Goethe, 1749–1832, German writer and statesman.
11. Gordon, M. (2005) *Roots of Empathy: Changing the World Child by Child.* Toronto: Thomas Allen Publishers, p.9.

Reinforcement Inventory

The Reinforcement Inventory is available to download and print from www.jkp.com/catalogue/book/9781785921438.

All of the items on this inventory are those that are likely to bring pleasure, peace or joy to a child. Check those items and see which ones will be more effective. Some of them will not apply.

Child: _____

Date: _____

Person completing form: _____

	Not at all	A little	A fair amount	A lot	A great deal
Hugs					
Quiet time					
Reading book/ shared reading					
Blowing bubbles					
Computer					
Dressing up					
Cars/wheeled toys					
Zoo/farm animals					
Colouring/ drawing/painting					
Cutting/sticking					
Construction/ building models					
Listening or dancing to music					
Playing outside					
Water/messy play					
Bat/ball/ football/ basketball, etc.					
Dinosaurs					
Watching DVD					
Other					

Index

Helen Garnett has a wealth of experience in teaching. Initially working in the primary sector, she co-founded a preschool in 2005, where she developed a keen interest in early intervention and the positive effect this has on a child's development and progress. More recently, Helen has become an early years consultant, focusing her expertise on helping develop an early years curriculum for Riverston Group International, where early intervention is key, underpinned by relevant, research-based training. Helen now trains practitioners in the UK and overseas. Helen also writes articles for leading early years and parenting magazines.